PRAISE

MEMOIRS OF A SUBURBAN TROUBLEMAKER

"Ellen didn't always make lemonade when life handed her lemons. *Memoirs of a Suburban Troublemaker is* a humorous but brutally honest and thought-provoking look at living through some of life's hardest experiences: divorce, bullying, racism, suicide, misogyny, subjugation, insomnia, learning disability, drugs, death, depression, politics, parenting . . . you name it. A book club must- read!"

—Cynthia Shang
Community Leader and Software Engineer

"In *Memoirs of a Suburban Troublemaker,* Readers are presented with an intimate coming-of-age story against the backdrop of Reston, Virginia. The author overcomes both childhood and adult challenges, navigates friendships, and finds a sense of self in the world. Readers will find joy in Ellen's her personal story but will also find a space for reflection."

—Alex Campbell
Executive Director of the Reston Museum

"'*Memoirs of a Suburban Troublemaker*' is an engaging and relatable read in so many ways. Right from the first page, it is full of stories that range from sweet anecdotes to wild escapades, all set against the suburban backdrop of Reston, VA. Through her honest and witty storytelling, the author weaves in the deeper message of advocacy and social justice as she embarks on a quest to challenge the status quo and confront injustices."

—Shantha Ramachandran
Reston Resident and Friend

"There is a plethora of material to capture your attention these days, and this book definitely captures your attention from the start. Ellen's story makes you laugh out loud, then makes you say, 'Damn, girl' and reflect on my your own life in parallel with hers. This book is about Ellen's fierce determination to fight for vulnerable groups and stand up against injustices. We all struggle with our own flaws, and it's beautiful to see Ellen outlining her own."

—Mina Song Palkendo
Reston Resident, Global Citizen, and Family Friend

"This book will have you scratching your head at times and saying, 'Did she really do/say that?' (Yeah, probably.) *Memoirs of a Suburban Troublemaker is* less a confessional and more an homage to 'it takes a village'—in this case Robert E. Simon's New Town of Reston, which, as the first avowedly open community south of Mason-Dixon, provided a moving example to this suburban troublemaker what good trouble looked like."

—Robert Goudie
Reston Community Leader and Family Friend

"Reading Ellen's beautiful memoir made me feel like I was reading my own. After all, how many Jewish girls who were eight years old when their parents got divorced, were raised in the utopian planned community of Reston, Virginia, and grew to become extremely close with their sisters can there be? Apparently at least two. Ellen perfectly captures what it was like to be the daughter of loving but flawed parents, smack in the middle of the 1980s divorce boom and against the backdrop of a uniquely modern American hometown (one that is so unique that you realize it's somewhat weird but beautiful idiosyncrasies only as you move away and can see it more clearly in the rearview mirror). *Memoirs of a Suburban Troublemaker* is a touching and funny journey of rebellion, self-discovery, and ultimately, peace."

—Melinda Arons
Producer and Media Consultant

Ellen R.B. Smith

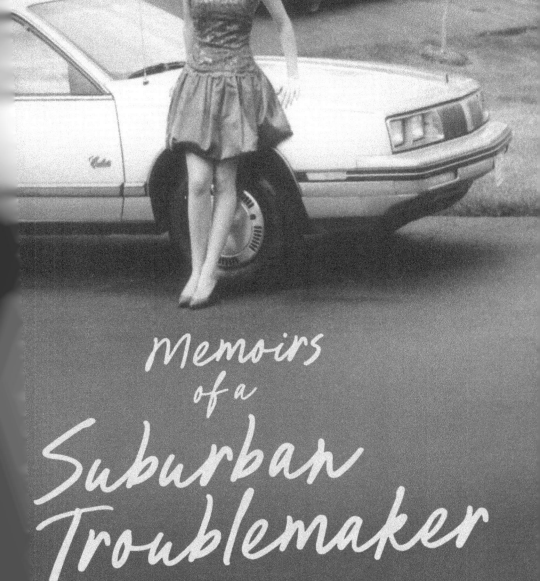

Memoirs of a
Suburban
Troublemaker

For permission requests, write to the publisher, addressed "Attention: Permissions Coordinator," at the address below.

Publish Your Purpose
141 Weston Street, #155
Hartford, CT, 06141

The opinions expressed by the author are not necessarily those held by Publish Your Purpose.

Ordering Information: Quantity sales and special discounts are available on quantity purchases by corporations, associations, and others. For details, contact the author at ellen.r.bernard@gmail.com.

Edited by: Malka Wickramatilakem, Connie Mayse, Nancy Graham-Tillman
Cover design by: Rebecca Pollock
Typeset by: JetLaunch

ISBN: 9781955985949 (hardcover)
ISBN: 9781955985956 (paperback)
ISBN: 9781955985963 (ebook)

Library of Congress Control Number: 2024907837

First edition, July 2024

Publish Your Purpose is a hybrid publisher of nonfiction books. Our mission is to elevate the voices often excluded from traditional publishing. We intentionally seek out authors and storytellers with diverse backgrounds, life experiences, and unique perspectives to publish books that will make an impact in the world. Do you have a book idea you would like us to consider publishing? Please visit PublishYourPurpose.com for more information.

*To my magical prince, my big boo bear,
and my baby snoop munchkin.
I love you to Uranus and back, times infinity.*

TABLE OF CONTENTS

PART 5

AUTHOR'S NOTE

Dear Reader,

    The contents herein is accurate and meticulously presented to the best of my ability. However, some of the events have been changed or embellished for the sake of the story, and in consideration of privacy certain names and identifying particulars have been altered. It has taken me slightly over a year to delve deeply into my collection of mementos to paint an authentic picture of my history. I hope you enjoy my flawed life story, which has been enriched by all the people who came to Reston, Virginia, a suburb of Washington, DC, to seek a better place to live. Thank you for giving me your time.

Love,

Ellen

FOREWORD

On July 27, 1975, I was eight days from my 25th birthday and two days late from my due date to deliver my first born. Ellen was a perfect baby and a complete joy to raise, at least until the age of 13. I was fortunate to be a stay-at-home mom for the first eight years of her life. She was the first beloved granddaughter of the Bernard Clan, but generated little interest from the Curl Clan, not a surprise considering that none of them liked themselves, let alone a new addition.

At the time, Ellen was the greatest gift and achievement of my life, and I'm still enormously proud of her and her accomplishments. That said, I would not wish her teenage years on another mother, including her. Nothing prepared me for her antics and behavior from the age of 13, and sometimes even now.

Her perception of her troubled life is very different from mine. When her dad and I separated, she was sad but enjoyed the discovery of a new neighborhood and the many friends she made while enjoying the lasting friendships from the old neighborhood. She contends that her depression, anger, and acting out began with the divorce, when in fact it began with the remarriage of her father.

Regardless of our different opinions, I believe that Ellen has written a compelling memoir with very real insights into the dangers of high school bullying and the consequences of bad decision-making.

Ellen remains the life of every party, a personality that people from all walks of life will gravitate to while being a loving mother, wife, daughter, sister, and friend. She's always had strong opinions and convictions in her beliefs. She still possesses the voice of a song-bird and may yet become famous, if not for singing then certainly for her humorous writing style and ability to entertain the masses.

Kitty Bernard
Ellen's Mom

PREFACE

Memories are immortal. They're deathless and precise.
They have the power of giving you joy and perspective in hard times.
Or, they can strangle you. Define you in a way that's based more in other
people's tucked-up perceptions than truth.

—Viola Davis, *Finding Me*

This book is a love letter to my family, friends, and hometown.

As a nonpracticing, agnostic, Jew-"ish" person on a lifelong quest to end racism and anti-Semitism, I was fortunate to grow up in Reston, Virginia, a town that was literally created as a place of inclusion for all. When my kindergarten teacher played the album *Free to Be You and Me* by Marlo Thomas and Friends, it fell directly in line with my view of Reston: where the "shining seas" were the man-made lakes, the "river running free" was the creek behind our house, and the "green country" was the 1,350 acres of open space that Reston's founder and namesake, Robert E. "Bob" Simon, had set aside for its residents.

As Virginia's first open, integrated, and planned community, Reston was a safe harbor, and I truly believed in the peaceful, egalitarian lessons taught at my elementary school. But inevitably, life's harsh realities could not be shielded from me, and when they hit, they hit hard. My childhood went from idyllic to completely chaotic, seemingly overnight.

A picture documents my first sustainable memory: I'm three years old and holding up blue homemade Play-Doh-covered hands, sitting in a yellow highchair that matched the '70s iconic harvest gold appliances, dishware, and wallpaper of our kitchen in New Jersey. I can distinctly recall my point of view, opposite the camera, with my mom directing me to "Say cheese!" and then setting the camera down on the counter to stir her cauldron of blue sorcery.

If I didn't have physical evidence of this moment's existence, I would have never remembered it. When we recollect a particular incident from the past, our neural net mutates and the adjustment impacts the next recollection of the moment. Meaning, the next time you remember the event, you might not recall the original memory but instead what you remembered the previous time. Even the word itself, "re-membering," indicates a need to reassemble or reconstruct; to put things back together after being separated. This book is a collection of my memories. Some have been cemented by retelling the stories or pictures, and some have been contaminated, but they're all building blocks for the person I am today.

I was a curious, precocious, funny, and determined kid. The most difficult thing in my childhood was bedtime, because I had a serious and rare form of insomnia called . . . never sleep. My parents tried every trick in the book, but I would fight sleep tooth and nail. As a teenager, I spent my days and nights fighting everyone.

My parents' divorce was a traumatic turning point in my young life. I went from being a child who respected authority and followed the rules to someone who was in constant trouble for misbehaving, getting poor grades, drinking, using drugs, and for physical alter-cations. My parents were unusually forgiving and compassionate. Despite their exceptional capacity for forgiveness, offering me all the grace they could muster, I remained the epitome of trouble.

PART

I

TROUBLEMAKER,

/ˈtrəbəlˌmākər/: noun: A person who habitually causes difficulty or problems, especially by inciting others to defy those in authority.

CHAPTER ONE

TELEPHONE POLES

I saw the telephone pole
When it hit me
The radio was playing
Sinéad O'Connor

The stop sign came quick
I noticed it after, I
Passed it. Leaves were
Everywhere

October 31st, 1:00 a.m.
I was lost, it was dark
My windshield wipers
Were on high

The beautiful voice
Never stopped singing

The door went
Concave

Glass was all around
I was trapped
The passersby would stare
But no one stopped

Except the police

—Ellen, age 17

In my 'tween years, I experienced one fight after another. If I wasn't
fighting with my parents, I was fighting with friends, random people,
and school administration. There were so few people who I felt stood
up for me. But from those who did, I learned we all need to have a
voice, and I realized that sometimes I could be that voice. I always
fought for the underdog. I got into trouble for it, but I knew I had
to stand up for those who couldn't stand up for themselves. I learned
about the Holocaust from my grandparents, including the injustices
they suffered because of their religion, and I knew there were a lot
of things in the world that were just wrong. How we treat people,
why we look down on someone, how we separate ourselves—these
were all acts of division, and I have spent my entire adulthood
trying to bring people together and create community. I have taken
my fight from the locker commons to the board room. John Lewis
famously said, "Speak up, speak out, get in the way. Get in good
trouble, necessary trouble." Trouble creates change.

In 2015, I connected with Reston's founder, Bob Simon, on a
party boat on Reston's Lake Anne. This was soon after Bob's 101st
birthday. He told us the secrets to his long life were daily morning
walks around Lake Anne and at least one gin martini at night. I

told Bob some of the stories I will share with you in the following pages. His last words to me were, "Don't ever change. Keep making trouble, Troublemaker." Bob passed away in the fall of that year. I would like to think those words of his were a kind of blessing—a blessing for these stories, a blessing for the shared experiences that we all have as we navigate life's highs and lows, and a blessing for all the troublemakers out there. Fight the good fight and see how we can make a positive change.

CHAPTER TWO

BLUE BEGINNINGS

My parents met at a Mobil service station in Sewell, New Jersey, when Mom, wearing hip-hugger jeans and a snug, ribbed knit sweater, brought her car in for maintenance. It was the '70s. Dad was handsome and a recent graduate from Penn State who was working there as a marketing representative and was smitten with Mom at first sight. The manager, Skip, told Mom the car would be ready the next day around noon. Skip called Dad and said, "Hiya, Jeff, if you want another shot to ask out Kitty Curl, be here at noon tomorrow."

The next day, Dad put on his best suit and tie and waited for Mom to arrive. He invited her to lunch and then out for a proper date the following Friday. Weeks went by before Mom found out that it had all been a setup, but by then she was already head over heels in love. Dad was intelligent, and charming, and my mom was so hot she could stop traffic. After a couple of months of dating, they moved in together, and two years later they got married on October 7, 1973.

Two years after that, and two days before she was meant to give birth, Mom woke up to severe contractions at 6 a.m. on July 27th. Once admitted to the hospital, she was given an enema, which was a huge discomfort. "Thankfully, they don't do that anymore," she said. I was born at 12:52 p.m. on July 27th, 1975, weighing seven pounds and four ounces. According to the story, she cried tears of joy for more than a week and continued to cry every time she gazed at my beauty.

Almost my whole family hailed from Philadelphia, the birthplace of my grandmothers, my parents, and me. I don't remember anything about Philly, the supposed city of brotherly love, as we stayed only for another six months. However, we ate scrapple, my favorite meat by-product, once a week for as long as I can remember. The first recorded recipes were likely created by my ancestors, who were German colonists that settled near Philadelphia in the 17th century. Dad's job with Mobil Oil moved us all over the Eastern Seaboard, landing us in Columbia, South Carolina, the same year Alex Haley's 1976 novel *Roots* and the subsequent television series were released.

We were in the thick of the South, and the neighbors couldn't get over how White people were negatively portrayed in that novel and movie. My mother was ostracized from her bridge club when they found out my father was Jewish. Our stint in racist Columbia lasted only six months, and my parents were happy to move back to Yankee territory—specifically Hampton, New Jersey, where, in 1978, my sister Julie was born. To this day I take great pleasure in telling everyone my sister was born in Flemington County, where some people think a runny nose is funny . . . but it's really *snot*.

When Julie was born, the whole family came to visit. "Mom Mom" and "Pop Pop" were my dad's parents. I assumed those were Jewish terms of endearment for grandparents; it wasn't until much later, in college, that I found out they were actually localized Philly terms. I don't remember who drove me to the hospital to see Julie after she was born, but I know both sides of my family were there to see my reaction to our introduction. I pointed to my sleeping sister's clear plastic crib through the window separating us from the nursery and said, "There she is!" According to everyone's account, I yelled, "Hey Julie! I'm your big sister! Mwah!" and kissed the glass. "Don't shout Dear," they said. "You'll wake all the babies."

After Mom and Julie came home from the hospital, Mom lay on the couch for hours, catatonic. I have no memory of this but must have known something was wrong because I handed Mom my favorite Winnie the Pooh stuffy. I wouldn't even let Julie near that one! My sad mom accepted the gift, tears rolling down her cheeks.

Only in my adulthood did I learn of Mom's postpartum depression after giving birth to Julie. I didn't know it when I was three years old, but Mom later said, "I'm not sure I would have ever snapped out of it without you."

CHAPTER THREE

RAVIOLI STANDOFF

I challenged bedtime and bathtime and tried to express my independence at any and every given opportunity. Julie was born a pleaser who got attention by calming everyone down. Everyone thought she would grow up to be a shrink. I, on the other hand, used my words and actions to get everyone to look my way. I loved Julie and, despite a few biting incidents, was happy to have a baby sister for company. I would even feed her marshmallows, not realizing they were choking hazards. Julie was a smart baby and figured out how to accept my gift of the gelatinous confection without dying. Mom found her using both hands to gnaw away on it, happy as can be, but I was scolded. Apparently, Mom didn't need help feeding the baby.

When I was three, I demanded ravioli every night, creating a standoff with Mom for months. Every night she would ask me, "What would you like for dinner tonight?" I'd give her the same exasperated answer: "Ravioli!" So every night for my dinner, she boiled the frozen sheets of square ravioli from Raffetto's with two pats of butter. I don't remember who gave in first, but we both distinctly remember spending hours in the bathroom. I cried on the toilet, and Mom sang softly to get me to "relax"— that is, to finally poop.

We didn't have car seats back in the '70s, which is a point highly contested by my mother, who swears she was so progressive that she'd purchased one eleven years before car seat laws were adopted in the US. But I remember traveling down the road in the velvety backseat of my parents' metallic brown, Delta 88 Oldsmobile. I'd often become car sick, especially when my parents smoked. The car was so massive it felt like we were driving inside a cozy living room, but once nausea took hold, there was no way to stop my stomach from turning somersaults except to throw up all over myself and parts of the backseat, making the car permanently intolerable. The only way to stave off nausea was to close my eyes, imagine myself seated in my favorite rocking chair, and rock my whole body back and forth.

Like a marching band's drum major, I felt personally responsible for keeping time. I'd listen to music and think its rhythm was solely accountable for keeping barf at bay. I imagine the people driving by must have thought I was having a seizure. While some kids sucked their thumb or stroke their faces, I rocked to self-soothe and didn't understand why or have the vocabulary to explain it until I read a bunch of baby books during my first pregnancy 36 years later. Self-soothing was a way to control my environment; to distract me from discomfort. Fortunately, our car rides and home were always filled with wonderful music. I especially loved jamming out to Stevie Wonder, Queen, Blondie, CCR, and Fleetwood Mac. And we listened to musicals like *Evita*, *Jesus Christ Superstar*, and *Cabaret*. Mom always said I could sing before I learned how to talk.

I went to Happy Face Nursery School in New Jersey so I could learn how to socialize. I had scores of friends there. It was also the scene of the crime where a boy stabbed me in the face with a paintbrush. Now only Mom can point out the scar. I had lots of neighborhood friends too, including Catherine, who lived across the street, and Denise, who wore a patch over one eye like a pirate. But the one I spent the most time with was Rico, who came from the exotic, far away, mystical land of Finland. We played friendly games like "I'll show you mine if you show me yours" while peeing in a bucket together. Rico taught me how to dig up earthworms from his backyard, eat onion grass directly from the ground, and lick the sweet nectar of honeysuckles by pulling the stem through the bottom. I often pondered eating a full meal off our property. I learned so many Finnish words that my mom thought I was fluent. Rico inspired me to always seek out friends from places outside the US to satisfy my endless curiosity.

Our house was the most popular in the neighborhood due to the free entertainment supplied by my dad's frequent tractor rides. So when it was time to move to Reston, Virginia, in the spring of 1980, I expected my friends to be a little bummed. Catherine cried like someone had died. Mom, who was equally surprised by her outburst of emotion, urged me to give her a hug and told her not to worry; we'd see each other again someday. Sorry we lied to you, Catherine. She may not remember me, but I would like to tell her that she made me feel extra loved that day and showed me how important it is to show people how you feel. I've tried to follow her lead.

CHAPTER FOUR

THE QUEEN
OF NEW JERSEY

I worshipped my father and thought he was the most handsome dad, with dark hair and eyes the color of ocean water—not the dirty brown Atlantic side, but like the Gulf of Florida's calm green waters, backlit by white sandy beaches. He stood six feet, three inches tall and wore a suit every weekday, like he'd just beat the house in Vegas. My heart soared when people said I looked like him. I wished he could have accompanied me at every first impression, like with the kids at school, so they'd see that I, too, could grow to be over six feet tall and important enough to wear fancy suits, just like him, and then maybe respect me, or at the very least, notice me. "This is my dad!" I'd say a little too loud and enthusiastically on the rare occasions he made an appearance. Dad was always working. However, Mom showed up to everything: the parent-teacher conferences, assemblies, choir concerts, special events, and every single extracurricular activity.

I knew my mother was way too talented and capable to just be a stay-at-home mom. As a young child, I bombarded her with questions to get to the bottom of what she should do with her life. "What did you want to be when you grew up?" I asked.

"A mom," she replied.

How dull, I thought. "What about music? You love music! What instrument did you play?" I asked, figuring she must have dreamed of being a rock star, like everyone else on the planet.

"The xylophone, but I wasn't very good. Not like you," she said, knowing flattery was the best stand-down elixir.

I loved having a mom who put my needs above her own, but I knew she had bigger dreams and certainly more to offer the world. My mom was the wise sage of the neighborhood—the other parents, especially those with the teenagers who were often my babysitters, would seek out my mom for advice. Mom just had a way of being there for everyone.

Dad and I bonded through the Indian Princess program. While it 100 percent exploited the traditions, customs, and culture of Native Americans, it was also our special time for just the two of us. Except, of course, for our "tribe": the ten other daddy–daughter pairs we met with once a month in alternating living rooms for "powwows." We passed a talking stick, engaged in staring contests, and told stories that patronized the Native American culture like a caricature, all while wearing blue felt headbands embroidered with yellow and red imagery of arrows and targets, teepees, trees, and fathers and daughters holding hands. My favorite game was "pull my finger," but I was alone in that endeavor.

I have only a handful of memories of being alone with my dad, like when he taught me to paint a wall. "Up and down in a straight line, and don't let it drip," he said. To clarify, this wasn't a metaphor to teach me karate; he just wanted help finishing our basement. We often went to Hechinger, which is now Home Depot. The smell of sawdust still triggers feelings of boredom and despair.

Dad always said the right things with the art of comedic timing. When he went away for work, I'd fish his dirty undershirts out of the laundry to hold while I slept. Mom kept offering them freshly cleaned. "No!" I'd shout, "I want daddy's smell!" which was a mix of his sweat and deodorant. This directly contributed to my armpit-sniffing obsession later in life. Mom's scent was undetectable, likely because we share the same DNA and overall personality.

Throughout my life, people used "Jewish" as an adjective to describe my features, which always piqued my metaphorical antenna. Maybe Judaism would have been a race had Jews not been exiled from everywhere they went, or murdered? Most of the time, I have the ability to fit in, and for me, Judaism was a choice, which not all Jewish people are granted.

My early knowledge of what transpired during the Holocaust planted ugly seeds deep into my psyche, as well as questions like, "If I time-traveled to Nazi Germany, would I be forced to wear a yellow star, and if so, how would they even know if I was Jewish?" "Also, why didn't God, who supposedly watches over all of us, intervene?" The simple answer (for me) was, "There is no God." Last, I wondered what the Holocaust victims felt while marching into those gas chambers, realizing no one was going to save them.

Due to rampant anti-Semitism, my grandfather (Pop Pop) was prohibited from giving a valedictorian speech at Drexel University in 1940. It wasn't until 30 years later, when he went back to Drexel to pursue his master's and again graduated at the top of his class (the same year my dad graduated from Penn State) that he was able to give his speech. He became a professor at Drexel and Rutgers, where he taught three times a week, in addition to his day job as an engineer for RCA.

I used to imitate my Pop Pop. If he was eating cherry yogurt, I would say, "Cherry is my most favorite flavor." When I would ask him how old he was, he would say, "We're about sixty-ish," to which I would respond, "Oh, well I'm about six-ish!"

Pop Pop could recite the US presidents in chronological order, as well as sing many national anthems from across the globe in his beautifully clear singing voice. He loved to stand about a foot away from the television, hands on his hips, in a room full of people trying to watch it. Mom Mom would shout, "Bill! You're in the way!" or "Bill, did you take your pills?" Mom Mom always kept a close eye on Pop Pop, eventually even putting a lock on the fridge, which may have extended his life 50 years longer than his weak heart and diabetes would have allowed.

Mom Mom (Marti) wore Emeraude perfume her whole life to feel closer to her mother Florence, who died from a botched hysterectomy when Marti was only 10 years old, and her youngest brother had died of pneumonia two years prior to that. She always had half pieces of spearmint gum in her pocketbook because she would split a piece of gum in half and give half to me, saying, "You have a small mouth, just like mine." To this day, I have spearmint gum in my purse and a bottle of Emeraude perfume to remind me of her.

Mom Mom lived to be 96 years old and was the epitome of fairness, but she had to suffer the predicament of watching everyone else in her generation die, including her husband, her siblings, and all her friends. Although she never told me I was her favorite, despite my relentless begging and pleading, she always made me feel special by lavishing me with unconditional love. Sometimes she called me her "angel," but more often than not, I was *mashugana*, which is Yiddish for "crazy." She loved to pinch my *tuchas* and supposedly found tomatoes and potatoes when she scrubbed behind my ears with a washcloth.

I have the most vivid memories of sitting in Mom Mom's lap and playing with the wrinkles on her neck and her tissue-paper-thin skin covered in freckles and bulbous veins, which were springy and fun to push. I played for hours on the weirdly placed pipes coming out of her yard. I imagined they were castles, and I was the Queen of New Jersey.

CHAPTER FIVE

RESTON AND THE PEGASUS

In 1980, my father's employer, Mobil Oil, relocated its headquarters from New York City to Merrifield, Virginia. Mobil's company's logo is a red Pegasus, a trademark that first emerged in Greek mythology. The majestic, winged horse magically appeared on mugs, clothing, and mail as well as in commercials and at gas stations. The idea that horses could fly validated my childlike optimism. I was devastated to learn it was just a Greek myth. Coincidentally, 1980 was the very same year Mobil decided to get into the real estate business by purchasing land from Gulf Oil in Reston, Virginia. This meant my dad's job, and we, would be moving.

"I don't do Reston!" were the words expressed by my parents' White male realtor. He continued, "If you want to see it that badly, I'll refer you to someone else." Reston was heavily advertised for being affordable (even with 13 percent interest rates) and convenient. But it also advertised a commitment to welcoming folks of all races and socioeconomic backgrounds, meaning no restrictions for sales to Black Americans. Reston was established in 1964, when an open community ran in opposition to accepted practices of the times in a red, confederate state—pre-fair housing laws, pre-*Virginia vs. Loving*, and pre-Civil Rights Act.

After searching several other affluent neighborhoods, my dad recalls choosing Reston for its 55 miles of bike paths, which we subsequently used to get to playdates, sports practice, and convenience stores. My parents were also enticed by the concept of living in Virginia's first planned community.

Like many other streets in Reston, Tanbark Drive was filled with new families looking for a place to plant their roots. My parents chose the neighborhood for its proximity to Terraset Elementary, Langston Hughes Intermediate, and South Lakes High School. All three were located across South Lakes Drive, the only street between our neighborhood and the campus of the three schools, which were situated within the same city block.

As the moving truck was being unpacked, a little girl watched our house from across the street, musing to her mother, "Mom, I think they have two little girls my age. Can we go outside to meet them?" Jaqueline Bernadotte took the hand of her daughter, Audrina, and walked over to initiate our friendships, already written in the stars. Audrina and I found so much more in common than our age and features. We, the only two Jewish girls in a predominantly WASP-y neighborhood, instantly became best friends; faithless, but nonetheless Jewish. Mom and Jaqueline hit it off as well.

Our house on Tanbark Drive was a blue single-family colonial, tucked away on a treed lot that included a private dock on Lake Audubon. It was a picturesque neighborhood, and we were a standard nuclear family, surrounded by other nuclear families. However, we had one neighbor two houses down who never said what he did for a living, just that he worked "for the government." Every time he went out of town, someone was assassinated. Dad, and everyone else, assumed he was a hit man for the CIA. Not a far-fetched occupation for a man living in the suburbs of Washington, DC.

Audrina and I made our friendship official. "Blood Sisters forever!" we chanted as we stabbed a needle into our fingertips and ceremoniously touched them together like Elliott and ET. We made up songs together, a series of snapping and clapping inspired by Billy Joel's "The Longest Time," and we performed them for our parents and friends. Audrina had beautiful chestnut brown hair that spilled down her back in perfect springy spirals. Jacqueline would get upset when she didn't wash it every day and wear it down. I didn't curry any favor with Audrina's mom when I took it upon myself to chop off her beautiful locks in one pretend "hair salon" appointment on the backyard picnic bench.

Being with Audrina was like living next door to my conscience. Remember those old cartoons with an angel on one shoulder and a devil on the other? I could always hear her soft voice in my head asking, "Do you really want to do that?" any time I sat on the precipice of making a bad decision. She learned quickly not to fall for my troublemaking antics, and she liked structure, rules, and figuring out why people do the things they do. She loved arts and crafts, like me. Unlike me, she was highly fashionable. I drove my mom crazy with clashing outfits of striped tops and plaid pants. Audrina took ballet lessons for years and still carries that gracefulness in her bones. I took tap for one season and gave up when I failed to master the "coffee grinder" move.

I convinced the neighborhood girls to join my underwear parade down Tanbark's sidewalk, where we marched naked, save for the pairs of Wonder Woman, Care Bear, Smurfette, and Princess Leia panties we each had on. We raised batons and Fourth of July flags (the only props we had on hand) and cheered, "This is a free country! Underwear is up to you!" until a parent showed up with towels and said, "It's inappropriate to walk around in your underwear." But I was the leader and got everyone to join me. I was making my presence known and it felt good.

CHAPTER SIX

SANTA'S BUGGER

When Julie and I were children, religion was more of an assumption. My parents had decided to raise us Jewish even before we were born, mainly because Dad grew up in a Reform Judaism home, and my mother's parents (a Yankee Catholic and a Southern Baptist) could never come to terms with the right religion for their seven living children. Passover Seders were spent with Dad's family, while Easters and Christmases were spent with my mother's.

Other than the Bernadottes across the street, I didn't know any other practicing or nonpracticing Jews. I reasoned that if Audrina was to be spared the pomp and circumstance of a formal Jewish upbringing (Sunday and Hebrew School, bat mitzvah, confirmation, and Jewish weddings), then so should I.

Most of the kids on our street went to catechism school, or CCD. I didn't understand why I was denied entrance to this seemingly elite and popular club, but I got a lesson anyway. According to the CCD kids, not all holidays were to be celebrated by everyone. Easter, Christmas, Ash Wednesday, and Good Friday were solely for

Christians, and the same delineation was true for Jewish holidays such as Rosh Hashanah, Yom Kippur, Passover, and Hanukkah. It was a choice where you must pick a side, just like voting, with only two boxes to check and a "write in" section that no one takes seriously. Schools didn't recognize Jewish holidays. There weren't any fun projects like there were for every other commercial and Christian holiday. Don't even get me started on Christmas music.

My sister and I understood the power of religious achievement as onlookers of the extravagant family bat and bar mitzvahs, but only Julie pursued Hebrew school. I went to Northern Virginia Hebrew Congregation's Sunday school twice. The first time, we made braided challah bread from scratch, and I thoroughly enjoyed it. The second time, I noticed how perfectly the other kids could recite the Hebrew alphabet, whereas I didn't even know the four simple letters on a dreidel—nun, gimel, hay, and shin—which made me hate myself. That was the end of my time at Hebrew school.

Anyone with freckles and braces reminded me of my older, male Jewish cousins whom I worshipped and adored—Brad, Scott, and Teddy. I fashioned paper clips into "retainers" and never wore sunscreen, hoping a freckle would magically appear, just to be like them. Before I learned to read, Passover meant hours of food deprivation in exchange for storytelling from the Haggadah, which tells the ancient (fifth century BCE) story of the Jews being freed from slavery in Egypt. It's when I discovered that parsley dipped in saltwater is surprisingly delicious and can settle a rumbling, starving tummy. And it's when I learned about participation—I just had to sing the repetitive lyrics to "Dayenu" along with its catchy tune, which was very easy to pick up, even for a non-destined-to-be-famous rock star.

When I was five, my mom sat me down at the top of the stairs and said, "I'm going to tell you a little secret, but you can't tell anyone because you don't want to ruin the fun for other children. Santa Claus was made up so parents can bribe their children to behave throughout the year." This was bad news. There was no escaping Christmas, a holiday rooted in American culture by the news, schools, media, and every person in my life. Anything Christmas-related made me feel isolated and excluded. Why did I have to endure the burden of this big secret? Why was I the only one denied lavish presents and the opportunity to experience that feeling of giving, along with the Christmas spirit? I wanted to feel the pure bliss and ecstasy that the made-for-TV movies all promised. Mom could tell I was bummed and tried to console me with yearly visits to her mother, who we called Bugger. At Grandma Bugger's house, fake Santa left me a gift each year, usually plaid pants or a denim purse.

Visiting Bugger also meant seeing my cousin Shannon. Shannon was just a toddler when she named my grandmother "Bugger." Her real name was Marie. Marie used to pinch Shannon's cheeks and say, "You little bugger!" So one day when Shannon's mom, my Aunt Patsy, was getting Shannon in the car to go to Marie's house, Shannon wailed, "I want to go to Bugger's house!" And the name stuck.

Shannon was two years older than me, and neither of our families took many vacations. Visiting each other was as close to a holiday as we could get. We knew we had crossed state lines by the road turbulence due to neglected potholes. "We're in Jersey now!" my parents would eke out in vibrating voices. Shannon would wait, peering impatiently out the living room window until we arrived. After being cramped in the car for three hours, I was already halfway out of the car before it stopped, sprinting across Bugger's yard into Shannon's waiting arms. We would shriek, as little girls do, as we barreled toward each other. Our hugs would be epic, swinging each other around like long-lost lovers in a movie.

CHAPTER SEVEN

IT'S ELECTRIC, DO DOODLE-DO DO DO!

Moving to a new town is never easy, and I was trying my best to fit in. We moved over the summer, two months before my fifth birthday, when Terraset, my future and futuristic elementary school, offered a tour to rising kindergartners. Terraset was the first underground school ever with solar panel electricity and heating!

On my first day, the other kindergarten kids laughed at the way I said "crayons," "water," and "bathroom"; it sounded like "crowns," "woodur," and "bafrooms" when the words came from my mouth. The kids would circle around me on the playground, waiting for me to say something else funny or different. It didn't take long to ditch my Philly accent, but it rears its cheesesteak, hoagie, scrapple-loving head when I'm angry, drunk, or in direct contact with my cousins.

I didn't like my first name when I was young. Ellen sounded like an old lady's name, but I loved my middle name, Rachael, so much so that I named everything else Rachael, including my grandmother's cat, my favorite stuffed animals, and "Rachael checkers," the new term I had coined for the yellow-and-white gingham pattern on my bedroom curtains, canopy bed, and comforter.

"Why couldn't you have named me something cute like Julie, or any name that ended in an 'i-e' or 'y'?" I asked Mom, waxing poetic about all the well-liked girls in my class named Katie, Becky, Amy, Emily, and so on.

"Well, I tried to name you Zelda, but your father turned me down," Mom said, giggling. "Plus, I've always loved the name Ellen. You'll appreciate your name when you get older, I promise."

She was right, but I tucked the name Zelda away as something portent. I didn't know what was coming at the time, but the imminent birth of my alter ego needed a name.

In first grade, I became so boy crazy I made a sign that said, "I love you, Tarak Knoble!" and held it up for Tarak and the whole class to read. He turned bright red and replied, "You spelled my name wrong." I then made a game of spelling his name in a million silly ways to hide the embarrassment from the rejection I felt. Everyone laughed except my teacher, Mrs. Dockery. She was the first Black woman I'd ever met and, subsequently, loved.

In second grade, there was a pretty girl named Nadine who was extremely gifted at soccer and whose mother worked as a crossing guard for our school. At recess, all the boys fought to get her on their respective teams, while the rest of us girls watched enviously from the sidelines. Nadine inspired me to try soccer in Reston's house league. As the only girl on the Scorpions team, the coach, who was the father of a fellow teammate, kept yelling, "She's a door, not a window! Go around!" in his Colombian accent each time the boys kicked a ball directly into my face or body. As with tap dancing, I lasted only one season.

I liked to play practical jokes on Mom in the mornings. "I told you to get dressed twenty minutes ago! Why are you still in bed?" she'd say. Then I'd throw off the covers to reveal my fully and appropriately clothed-for-school body. When she'd say, "Get your ass out of bed, Ellen!," I'd then lie face down with my butt in the air until she came back into the room. Sometimes I'd get a laugh, but most of the time I was just in trouble. And late for school.

Every kid had allegiance to their neighborhood pool, which was the embodiment of everyday summer life. I joined the swim team the summer I turned six, which gave me a bit of confidence in my abilities, finally. My mom was my biggest champion. "I think she might be part fish; she's faster than a shark!" she'd brag to anyone who would listen. "Mom, I'm a mermaid," I'd say, sprinkling Morton's salt in my bath after watching *Splash* for the 853rd time. But alas, my legs never turned into orange-scaled fins.

I was so proud of my Ridge Heights Pool blue racing suit with the white stripes running down the side that I wore it the entire summer. I also believed chlorine was powerful enough to satisfy all my hygienic needs and used it as an excuse to replace showering. My absolute favorite memories are of watching the shock and disapproval cross our parents' faces as we chanted in unison to the following tactless cheers:

"Ice cream, ice cream, banana split!
We think your team sucks like . . .
. . . Shift to the left, shift to the right,
stand up, sit down, fight, fight, fight!"

And
"U! G! L! Y! You ain't got no alibi.
You're ugly, you're ugly,
And that's your mama's fault!"

And my most favorite:
"Ice cold beer
Makes me want to cheer,
Ice cold wine
Makes me feel fine,
Ice cold duck
Makes me want to
SWIM FAST!"

Mom had the most coveted volunteer role thanks to her beautiful speaking voice and charming intonation: swim meet announcer. She would be perched on a balcony with a microphone and a giant PA system while other volunteers, called runners, would deliver information for her to read aloud into the mic. This gave her the best view of the pool.

Julie was about to have her first race and was so nervous, her stomach was in knots. Her face wore a post-apocalyptic, all-the-oceans-have-dried-up expression. Mom told me to go to the starting line and comfort Julie, since she had to stay on the balcony. "Rub her tummy and tell her everything is going to be okay," she instructed.

I ran down to the pool's edge where Jules (how I often referred to Julie) was standing worried and anxious. I put one arm around her shoulders and rubbed her tummy with the other, as directed. I looked up at Mom and gave her a wink, then whispered in Julie's ear, "You can do this. Don't embarrass me."

The starter fired his blank gun. Julie hesitated, and I moved my hand from her shoulder to the middle of her back and pushed her into the water. She belly-flopped and sank a little, but she slowly emerged from underneath the surface and struggled across the pool, drowning intermittently. I met her at the other end to congratulate her, but she swatted my open arms away, still upset over the push

CHAPTER EIGHT

LET'S GO TO FUNERALS!

Third grade was the year of death. The death of a classmate, the death of my Aunt Caroline, the death of my parents' marriage, and the death of my academic life.

Kinsley Cain was the most sought-after playmate in the entire class on the days that doctors cleared her to come to school. Notified the day prior to her arrival, our teacher warned us, "No roughhousing on the playground," even though Kinsley's frailness was plain as day. Her skin, seemingly made from eggshells, revealed every little blue vein. Her angelic face was framed by shiny chestnut hair in the popular bowl-cut style, just like almost everyone else's. She was underweight and always congested, with labored breathing. However, she was so thrilled to be at school, her positive attitude outshined the severely debilitating cystic fibrosis she'd inherited. It was like a bad dream that one day she might wake up from, but she never did.

Kinsley's death was the first time I experienced a loss within the Reston community. I'd known her since we were in kindergarten; she was my friend. When our teacher broke the news, all the kids burst into tears, except for me. I sat stone-faced, in complete awe of the lack of emotional inhibitions of my fellow classmates who were bawling their eyes out. I look back on this moment and wish I'd just let myself experience the full impact of grief instead of keeping it bottled up. I worried that if one tear slipped out, the floodgates would open and I wouldn't know how to close them. Kinsley died peacefully in her sleep, surrounded by her family in the hospital, where she spent more than two-thirds of her short life.

My parents didn't take me to the funeral. They didn't take me to my Aunt Caroline's funeral either. Caroline was Mom's youngest sister, who died in a car accident. I was witness to the enormous influence her death had on my mother but was prevented from experiencing the grieving process alongside her. I feel like I missed out on an opportunity to say goodbye to my Aunt Caroline and my friend Kinsley and to show support for the living who loved them.

Both Aunt Caroline's and Kinsley's deaths were true tragedies. Little did I know that another death was looming ahead that school year: the death of my parents' marriage.

CHAPTER NINE

THE CURSED MEZUZAH

I experienced the happiest moment of my childhood at six years old. I heard music coming from downstairs, hours after my parents had put us to bed. Fleetwood Mac's *Rumours* album was blasting from the new stereo system, perched inside custom cabinets and racks that my dad had proudly built. Dad's carpentry skills were so legendary, I frequently compared him to Jesus.

I crept downstairs, barefoot, and found my parents cuddling and laughing on our white, wool, woven couch. On the coffee table in front of them lay a paper plate filled with piles of marijuana, tweezers, and some rolling papers. They spotted me, crouched behind the armrest, and pulled me onto their laps. Feigning anger and shaking me a bit, Mom growled, "What are you doing? Why are you still awake?"

I smiled and laughed at her spot-on impersonation of Cookie Monster and replied, "Couldn't sleep. What are you doing?" My head was nodding in the direction of the paper plate. I was wide-eyed and curious.

"Making cigarettes," Dad answered.

I asked if I could help.

"No, Sweet Pea, but we'll make you a sandwich," Mom said cheerfully.

Sandwich-making fit right into my plan of delaying bedtime. Any excuse to avoid lying in bed alone in the dark was good enough for me. My mom propped some pillows against the headboard for me so I could eat in a reclined position. They both stood next to the bed, looking down at me with the goofiest adoring smiles on their faces. They never looked this cheerful and rarely this happy with me. Normally if I snuck up on them, they were never this pleasant about it. Once, I pulled out all the paper from inside our new mezuzah, a small, sacred Jewish decorative case placed on the threshold of the entrance to a home, meant to bless and sanctify a living space. In fact, the word *mezuzah* means "doorpost" in Hebrew. My vandalism of the mezuzah, according to them, was blasphemy resulting in seven years of bad luck. This seemed like a ridiculous and made-up superstition. Little did I know.

But that night, my mom stroked my hair and my dad massaged my feet. I felt so loved. They made jokes and reveled in the beauty of their own creation—me, not the sandwich. Tears of joy sprang into my mom's warm, lake-water-colored eyes, eyes that are just like mine but with more green algae rippling around the edges. After I ate the sandwich, they took turns kissing me goodnight and said, "Nighty Night! Sleep tight. Don't let the bed bugs bite" before walking out of the room, still giggling like school children. I finally fell fast asleep, despite the talk of bed bugs.

In third grade, I experienced the saddest moment of my childhood. It was a Saturday, and my dad was sitting on the full-sized bed that was covered in a yellow-and-white quilt that had been handmade by my mother. Each 12 x 12-inch square had a different pattern or picture stitched inside. He sat so he could be eye-level with my sister and me. We'd been summoned to the guest bedroom, deliberately chosen for its neutrality, by my mother, who ushered us in by saying, "Daddy wants to talk about something important." She then left the room, knowing full well how traumatic sharing the upcoming news with a pair of eight- and five-year-olds would be, but she left a sliver of space between the door and frame to eavesdrop from outside.

My mom's youngest sister, Caroline, the only blonde, blue-eyed girl of the bunch—recently engaged and only 20 years old—had died a year earlier in a car accident, and my parents had been fighting tremendously ever since. Did this have something to do with that?

My dad held his head in his hands, sobbing uncontrollably. When he finally gained composure, he told us he needed to live somewhere else because our mother wanted a divorce. What? This made no sense. We started to ask logical questions like, "Why? Don't you love us anymore?" when Mom swung the door back open to chastise him.

"Get a grip, Jeff!" she said, then bent down to talk to me directly. I was hysterical; there was no pretending to be brave in that moment. "We love you both very much. This is not your fault," she said. Then she rolled her eyes at my father, who picked up his suitcase and descended the flight of stairs down to our foyer. I chased after him, but Mom took the lead to block the door in front of me.

Dad was already outside getting into his car. I fumbled to unlock and open a window, then screamed out, "No! Daddy, please come back!" I was yelling at the top of my lungs. *Maybe he can't hear me*, I thought. *I have to scream loud enough and then maybe he will turn around and end this misery*. "Don't leave, Daddy! Please come back!" I cried inconsolably. Never once did he look back. Never once. My heart broke and never quite healed, leaving me terminally fractured.

Everything was awful. I just wanted to go back to the way things were before he abandoned us. Grief and anger were my only companions now. I spent my days looking for a self-destruct button. I started acting out, attacking my sister, and zoning out like a space cadet at school, unable to retain or pay attention to anything but my own sorrow, especially around math time. Everyone else seemed to be thriving, making my melancholy more apparent and perverse.

I found myself twice a week in the office of a child psychologist named Dr. Farber. This lasted around a year and may have helped, although as a child, it just felt punitive and I couldn't see it.

Dad found an apartment almost immediately. Mom, Julie, and I continued living in our house on Tanbark Drive for an additional six months, but once it was sold, our holidays became broken affairs. Mom moved us into a townhouse in Hearthstone Court, and we'd half pack our suitcases to stay with Dad on the days he had custody. Our new home with Mom was located farther from the school and deeper in the woods than we had previously been. Our townhouse was the end unit in our row and backed up to a giant hill, which was our path to school.

I wondered who had bought our old house. Would they realize the sounds of the lake monster stepping closer and closer to my bedroom at night were really just the sounds of a ticking clock? It took me years to figure that one out.

The family that moved in had a girl my age with brown hair and a younger sister. Her name was Donna Martin. She was the new me. My room was now her room. I worried she'd take Audrina away too, so I made sure to stay in constant contact to prevent this from happening.

We'd visit Audrina and her parents somewhat regularly. Each time I passed my old house, I'd see the enormity of the evergreen tree that my parents had planted together just two years earlier. I was envious of that tree—it had survived blizzards and torrential downpours and always came out on the other side. My family was falling apart, and all I wanted was for us to be strong like that tree, to come out on the other side, together. I knew the Martins would cut that tree down, and without fail, they did. The tree that had stood so majestically, representing happy times and my parents loving each other, became a heap of chopped up branches and mulch. I felt the way that tree looked.

Once I found an electric guitar hidden in the woods behind Dad's apartment on Shire Court and brought it home. Dad said, "Sorry honey, but it was definitely stolen. It doesn't belong to us, and we need to give it to the police." He wouldn't even let me play it! I was devastated and believed he squandered away my only chance to teach myself how to play guitar. I didn't commit the crime, and in my opinion anything found in the woods should be fair game, just like when Mom had to go back for our bikes after my accident. Nothing made sense, and it seemed that every time I tried to take a step in the right direction, I was boomeranged back 10 steps in the wrong one.

I was intensely aware of the monetary setback our move to Hearthstone Court inflicted, but it wasn't just the socioeconomic downgrade that bothered me. I hated leaving the bubble of familiarity, the comfort, and the codependent life of having a stay-at-home mom. I loved having my best friend right across the street and missed the convenience of our daily adventures. The move impaired our entire network of friends, our daily routines, and the philosophical construct of "family."

The most blaring hit in the gut was our living conditions. Tanbark's contemporary style single-family house was in complete contrast with the drab, musty-smelling townhouse of Hearthstone Court. Infested with large camel crickets capable of leaping three feet high, our basement was dreary, and our home lacked the landscaping present in the neighboring houses. The decline in our circumstances was unmistakable to all around us. Though Reston was a welcoming town for all races and income levels, kids always knew where you fit in on the matrix—not just from where you lived, but by what you wore, the car your parents drove, and what people said about you.

My parents both worked long hours and were exhausted. Each seemed to be hanging on by a thread, and I didn't want to be the culprit of any additional fatigue. I tried to reserve serious ailments for doctor visits. So when a plantar wart was growing inside the bottom of my foot, I decided to take the unsightly matter into my own hands and control what popped up on my skin by scratching it off. I sat on the floor of Dad's dining room and dug the wart out of my foot with the tine of a kitchen fork. It was difficult since it had grown what looked to me like tentacles, but I was really proud of myself for solving a problem without medical assistance. I even threw out the fork afterward for sanitation purposes.

The loss of wealth (or perceived wealth) and imminent drop in future resources made what was once fun—like shopping for clothes and groceries and signing up for sports, summer camps, and dance classes—now an argument, and we'd bicker about money until someone (usually me) ended up in tears or grounded. Mom used to tend to my every whim. She used to make my lunches with such care, methodically filling celery sticks with cream cheese and strategically placing slivers of green olives stuffed with red pimento. Every color of the rainbow was represented in these spreads. She also used to sew Halloween costumes from scratch and was so good at it she taught all the kids from the Tanbark neighborhood to sew. Audrina still has the pillows!

Losing Mom's attention for her new day job felt like I was losing an appendage. I couldn't do anything without her. The days of having an involved PTA parent, like when she came to school for Pioneer Day to watch me demonstrate the do-si-do and promenade square dances and made the class quilt with each student's personalized section of fabric, were over.

CHAPTER TEN

Boobs By Osmosis

My dad's two-bedroom apartment on Shire Court had rust-colored carpets, sliding glass doors, and floor-to-ceiling windows in the back. The slanted ceiling gave the apartment a contemporary feel. At first, Julie and I didn't need the extra bedroom because we slept with Dad. All of us seemed to want as much time with each other as possible. Snuggles abounded, and Dad was more sensitive to us because he'd been lonely too, but that didn't last very long.

His first girlfriend, Joni, had blue eyes and thick, dark, curly hair. Dad brought her with us on a trip to visit Mom Mom and Pop Pop in Florida, but their house wasn't big enough for everyone, so Dad and Joni got a hotel room nearby and stayed there the entire week. I begged my grandparents to take Julie and me in. I was desperate to be around happy adults who loved each other and who loved me. My need to secure a place in a family with two parents was my top priority. The yearning to have my family back, the nuclear family that we had always been, was such a visceral desire that it superseded any inkling of empathy I could have had for my parents, who I knew were struggling; they both seemed stressed, tired, and grumpy all the time. Mom Mom turned down my pleas, trying to comfort me by saying, "No honey, that won't work because your parents would miss you too much." Yeah, right.

Dad's next girlfriend, Deloris, had a daughter named Elizabeth, who was legally blind. One afternoon, Julie and I were riding in the backseat with her on our way home from a hot air balloon show when Julie asked, "Is Elizabeth going be our new sister?" An awkward silence followed.

There were other women in between, but I didn't get to meet them all. Both my parents were good-looking people, and it made sense that they would date. I was just hoping that they would realize how unhappy *I* was and get back together, but neither of them took my metaphorically overambitious bait.

I couldn't process my feelings of loneliness and anger. Hormones affected my mood like the stock market. I was angry when everyone else pretended life was great. I was also jealous of my sister's ignorance. She didn't remember what life was like before the divorce, and her relationship with Mom was only strengthened by the split because now she had all of Mom's attention. Watching them ooh and ah over each other made me physically ill. I avoided their affections and repelled tenderness at all costs. When my mom and sister would cuddle together on the couch, I'd take the chair and grab my own blanket. I resented their peaceful relationship and decided to deprive myself of all human contact. Disguising my vulnerability was exhausting, but I was desperate to be in control over my life. I wanted my family back, but instead I pushed everyone away just so I could feel like I was in the driver's seat. Being that I'm an extrovert, this was counterintuitive to my needs; the isolation made everything worse.

It wasn't just me pulling away. My dad's numerous girlfriends would drop veiled remarks insinuating that I was too big to sit in

Dad's lap. Except for greetings or farewells, I refrained from physical contact, maintaining a personal space that mirrored today's concept of social distancing before it became a widespread practice.

Dad was an executive at Mobil Oil when he met LeeAnn, who was a secretary in another department. LeeAnn passed Dad in the hallway and said in her sweet Kentucky accent, "Oh no! You're limping! Did you hurt yourself in the softball game last night?" Dad replied, "No, this is the way I walk." Embarrassed, LeeAnn went by his office later that day to apologize, and Dad asked her out on a date. The rest is history.

Before Dad married LeeAnn, she sent me and Julie cards in the mail for every holiday, even St. Patrick's Day and the Fourth of July. For birthdays, she'd make us the most elaborate cakes; knowing I loved Garfield, she painstakingly used frosting to complete, quarter inch by quarter inch, this fantastic replica of Garfield's face and body. And she gave me my first perm.

LeeAnn was also the only one who noticed how self-conscious I was about my swollen nipples and bought me a training bra and matching underwear with a sweet little pink-and-green flower print, which made me feel all grown up. And good grief, I really wanted boobs! Not necessarily big ones; any size would have done the trick. Like the misheard lyrics by the Pussycat Dolls, "When I grow up / I wanna be famous / I wanna be a star / I wanna be in movies / When I grow up / I wanna see the world / drive nice cars / I wanna have boobies."

Swollen nipples aside, I was falling behind on becoming a woman. As I got older, I did manage to spare myself from being brainwashed by the media, big-busted Barbie dolls, and airbrushed women in magazines and withstood the temptation to alter or augment my natural breasts. This was mostly because I'm too chicken-shit to cut myself intentionally in the name of beauty. The thought of having a foreign object inserted into my body, especially one that could leak or backfire and require follow-up surgery, terrifies me. However, when I was in third grade, I would have done ANYTHING for boobs.

Julie and I pretended to be detectives to scour through our parents' closets. Once we found an ounce of schwag—dirt weed—on the top shelf of Mom's bedroom closet. Her friend Rob Bandazo from high school had sent it to her in the mail. Rob always tried to stay in touch, even after he went to jail for selling drugs. In her memory box, Mom kept a picture of him wearing a white suit, just like Don Johnson in Miami Vice. Rob was an attractive, tan, Italian man. Mom always had an affinity for Italians, having grown up in an Italian neighborhood in South Philly. Rob gave me a rare 1975 buffalo nickel from the year I was born. I never met him, though.

In Dad's closet, we found about 50 *Playboy* magazines. I smuggled half into the bag I packed during one of the original school night custody splits: Tuesday through Thursday and every other weekend. Once at home (Mom's), I hung 30 naked booby pictures all over the walls of my room. Mom found them, called my dad immediately to cuss him out, and told everyone else I was hoping to grow boobs by osmosis.

Ethnic Pride Day at school was once again upon us, and I had completely forgotten to tell either of my parents. I was at Dad's when I suddenly remembered that it was the very next day, and I needed a costume to salute my heritage. Dad was furious and was about to phone my mom to complain when LeeAnn intervened, pulled her sewing machine out of the closet, and proceeded to turn a set of sheets into an outfit commemorating my (imagined and supposed) lineage of Cherokee Native American. I was really grateful to have someone sewing for me again.

For a while, I was the shortest girl in my class. I complained about a boy from school who called me short. Although I held the record in the flexed arm hang (the girl version of pull-ups) and my name was on the wall of the Terraset gym for the remainder of my elementary school career, being called short was a true insult and made me feel small and insignificant.

One evening, LeeAnn and I were sitting in the car at the mall, waiting for Dad and Julie to finish checking out. It was dark, save for a streetlamp casting a faint glow far off in the parking lot. LeeAnn sat in the passenger seat, and I could see only the silhouette of her perfect, former University of Kentucky homecoming queen profile from the backseat. She told me all the reasons why boys like short girls: "They like feeling in control, but really it's us in the driver's seat." Even though I was bummed about losing my recently acquired right to sit in the front seat—because when LeeAnn rode in the car, she always got shotgun—I appreciated the effort she made to try to make me feel better.

CHAPTER ELEVEN

THE BLOODY CORPORATE LADDER

After Mom and Dad's divorce, Mom got a receptionist role close to home at a company called Hunter Lab, which invented a technology to measure color. The office hallway was painted in a prism of colors that stretched from one side of the building to the other and was displayed through glass windows for all of Sunset Hills Road to see.

Mom was desperate to make more of her career than her parents had and worked very hard. However, if I got sick, she would come home for lunch and leave the office early to take care of me. She had the warmest and most loving bedside manner, unparalleled by anyone, but she was never as kind to herself.

She once woke me up, holding a washcloth to her face; it was soaked in blood. "Mom, what happened?!" I cried. She had slipped in my bathroom and split her lip on the edge of the tub.

"Get up, get dressed, and help your sister," she said sternly, ignoring my pleas to call a friend to help her.

"Let's call an ambulance! You're bleeding!" I begged.

"Get ready and help your sister!" she spat angrily.

I got up and did what I was told.

Mom had to leave before I was able to wake Julie. She drove herself to urgent care, where they gave her stitches and sent her on her way to make it to work on time—where she kept her head down to avoid questions. I was a nervous wreck all day.

In my opinion, it took Mom 11 years and a mountain of misogyny to work her way up the corporate ladder. She went from bookkeeping to accounting, then later became a marketing manager. In that role, the company's revenue went from $12 million a year to $28 million.

Mom's job sent her all over the country for trade shows. When she had to travel on weekends, I would have to spend the night at a friend's house. I hated staying at my friend Amelia's apartment. She always made me sleep on the floor of her bedroom so we could "be together." I didn't like sharing a room, especially when "being together" meant Amelia slept aloft on her bed while I was four feet below on the hard-ass floor.

Once, Amelia's mother came to say goodnight, turned on the lights, and caught me crying. When questioned, I told her I didn't want to talk about it, hoping she would just ignore me. Sleeping on the floor was a reminder that I didn't have a say in or control over anything. I never really dealt with the grief of losing my nuclear family, the only concept of family I had ever known. I was angry at my mom for kicking my dad out and getting a job, one that required her to leave me alone with nowhere else to go but Amelia's crappy apartment floor. I was mad at my dad for remarrying so quickly to start a new family. I was mad at everyone.

Mom took on another job as a fitness instructor a handful of nights a week to make extra cash, stay in shape, and continue her social life with Sue Krause. Sue was the owner of The Fitness Studio, a friend from Tanbark Drive, and a fellow divorcée. They were both running short on cash and were forced to sell their homes. Once, in the depths of financial discontent, they were drinking a bottle of Sutter Home White Zin when Sue found an advertisement in the newspaper for a mink coat. "I really want this mink coat! I deserve this mink coat!" Sue exclaimed. They wept with laughter. A mink coat was the furthest thing either of them could dream of buying.

When Mom came home from work, she'd spend hours sitting on our balcony staring off into the woods, alone with her thoughts. I kept thinking she wanted company out there, but she didn't. "I'm exhausted, Ellen," she'd say. "I just want to be alone because the silence helps me think." She was in the process of mentally excommunicating herself from her abusive family, though I didn't know it at the time. As a tween, I felt like she was excommunicating herself from me, and this was insulting. Why couldn't I remain her confidant like I was before the divorce? Also, it hurt that she didn't seem to care about what was going on in my life, which was quite a bit!

Once Mom realized she could make it without my dad and her family, she was ready to clean house and rid herself of any harmful relationships. Everyone deserves a mother who loves and cares for them, but Mom was the unlucky fifth child, born 15 months after a set of twins. She was unwanted, unplanned, and unloved by everyone. Though she did her best to stay under the radar, never complaining when she was cold, hurt, or uncomfortable, her mother continually schemed to get rid of her. Her father wasn't any better; he was violent and verbally abusive as well. Her time being in her own head while sitting on the balcony and gazing at the woods was her way of working through the trauma, but I didn't know this until I was an adult.

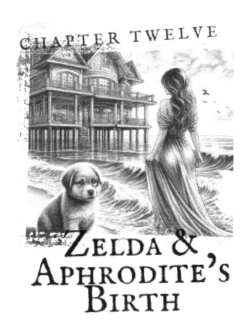

CHAPTER TWELVE

ZELDA & APHRODITE'S BIRTH

The day before my ninth birthday, Mom took me to Subway during her lunch hour to celebrate my entrance into the world. Standing in line, she said, "I can't believe my baby is turning nine! You're only one year away from being in double digits!"

The plan was to spend my real birthday at the beach with my friend Heidi from school. She had invited me to Duck Beach, North Carolina, with her family for a whole week. "One year and one day," I said, realizing this would be the first time I'd spend my birthday with someone other than my parents, the first time I'd go anywhere without my family, and, to add insult to injury, my first birthday after the divorce.

My smile faded and Mom asked, "Are you sure you want to go away on your birthday?" I wasn't, but I channeled the ability to impersonate myself and acted as if nothing were wrong. I tried to remember how much I loved the beach, and this was likely my only chance to go. Plus, I'd never been to the beaches of North Carolina, and money was so tight that Mom couldn't afford a party anyway.

When Heidi's dad pulled their packed station wagon into our parking lot, a feeling of unease swept over me. It was the same feeling, a sickness clutching my insides, that I had when I observed all the intact families of my cousins at the synagogue for their bar and bat mitzvahs. I felt inconsequential to my parents. Maybe I was too old for birthdays? Maybe they were just too busy trying to rip off the bandage of codependency and move on with their lives sans each other? Either way, one thing was clear: it was time for me to grow up.

The station wagon was filled to the brim with beach chairs, coolers, and a Sears clamshell storage cargo box on top. Heidi and I sat in the very back, facing the road. Heidi's sister, Alice, and her friend Carrie were in the back seat. The drive took four hours. Luckily, Heidi's parents didn't smoke, and we played the license plate game to distract me from motion sickness.

We arrived at an enormous, gray beach house on stilts, unloaded our belongings, and went upstairs to the kitchen on the top floor for a snack. Heidi and I then ran to the ocean as fast as we could. We were both strong swimmers, thanks to the swim team, though she was on the rival Newbridge team. We floated for hours in the calm surf, avoiding the ground to save the soles of our feet from shredding apart on the jagged rocks underneath us. Eventually, Heidi's parents called us inside for showers and dinner.

I tried to remember my manners, be polite, say thank you after every meal, and be tidy. I was so grateful to be included, and the oceanfront property gave me a new window into another world. This was the life I wanted! I needed to shake the troublemaker label given to me by so many.

I wanted to get invited back, but I had a serious problem: it hurt to pee. I didn't know why and was panic-stricken, terrified they'd think I was a bad guest, or worse, someone who ruined their vacation. So

I kept the fear that my vagina had inadvertently swallowed a jellyfish under wraps and stayed quiet, hoping it would go away on its own. It did, thank goodness—all I needed was to drink a glass of water. However, I will never forget sitting on that toilet, stifling a scream, wondering if my pee had somehow turned to acid.

My actual birthday was spent applying massive amounts of makeup in preparation for a photoshoot out on the balcony. Heidi wore conventional '80s makeup: blue eyeliner and mascara that matched her blue eyes, shimmery eye shadow, and neon-pink lipstick. I smeared a two-inch perimeter of iridescent purple eyeshadow around my right eye, like Pete the Pup from the Little Rascals.

On the last day of the trip, we all came back from the beach and were showering for dinner when Heidi's dad entered our bedroom without knocking. We were wrapped in towels, but Heidi went ape-shit. "Dad, you have to knock! We are getting dressed!"

He quickly retreated and yelled "Sorry!" on his way out.

I stood there motionless, in shock. I couldn't process the meaning of what had just transpired. In my house, we ran around naked all the time. I didn't realize I had anything to hide, but from that moment on I decided that I, too, shall be modest, which perplexed the hell out of my mom and sister when I was back home. Mom worried something more traumatic had happened when I refused to undress in a group setting, but she dismissed the thought because my strange modesty was always accompanied by cheerfulness and optimism. It wasn't until we drove to my college orientation that she finally asked, "Alright, what the hell happened on that trip?" I laughed and said, "I just realized how inappropriate it was to flash my friend's dad."

In fourth grade, I auditioned for district choir by sight-reading a few bars of music and a portion of the Star-Spangled Banner. Only eight kids (four girls and four boys) would be selected. More than half the school auditioned, and at the end of the day each name was read aloud over the intercom system. When my name was called, I jumped out of my seat, delighted beyond belief! I squealed and did a little booty dance after the announcement was over. A few kids clapped, one gave me a high five, but most stayed seated, either seething with jealousy or indifferent with boredom.

The day of rehearsal, Mrs. Luke fastened to my white shirt an index card with my name and "Soprano 1," the highest of the four standard singing voices. The bleachers were packed with hundreds of students from other schools. The process of elimination worked; we sounded amazing, and I had truly leveled up. Getting chosen confirmed my suspicion that I was finally good at something. It instilled a confidence in me that influenced my decision to minor in vocal performance in college and my audacity to steal the microphone every chance I could get.

At home, we finally got a piano, a used upright from Jordan Kitt's, which we positioned against our only exposed brick wall in the living room. Mom had saved every penny to get that thing. Playing piano was my favorite pastime. I got pretty good for an eight-year-old who initially learned to play on a neighbor's piano. However, I reached the pinnacle of my piano prowess by age 10. Jules and I had lessons, but those ended after a recital because of an aggressive, hairy, angry piano teacher (who we could barely afford) who pounded his gorilla hands on our fingers when we didn't play the right notes.

I didn't have Elton John's perfect pitch or his ability to play Mozart's "Rondo Alla Turca" after hearing it only once, but I could intone all the melodies of the songs I heard on the radio and got really good at playing "Heart and Soul" with my cousin Brad. There always seemed to be a piano around at all the bat and bar mitzvahs we attended together. I still wanted to be just like all my cousins, but instead of coveting the presence of braces and freckles, I now coveted the presence of parents.

On a snowy winter day, school let out two hours early. I had to walk to a sitter's house in a nearby neighborhood. Julie took the bus. Our memory of this place involved our food and beverage deprivation while the kids who actually lived in that house got all the snacks and apple juice their greedy hearts desired. Basically, everyone sucked royally and never shared their toys or wanted to play with us.

On that day, I was walking alone through the snow when two misanthropes, Steve O'Doyle and Courtney Donahue, started to follow me to the sitter's house. I knew Steve from school and our swim team, but I'd never talked to him and was surprised when he called out to me. His red hair and bright-green eyes popped in contrast to the winter wonderland surrounding us. "Wait up!" he said.

I turned and stopped to take in the tall, lanky shape of his build. His approach gained momentum with a terrorizing rush. He pushed me hard, knocking me to the ground. I felt the cold seeping into my body as he and Courtney pinned me down into the snow. Steve grabbed a wad of snow while Courtney secured my arms. I was paralyzed, unable to move any appendage, with the weight of Steve's knees smashing my airway into a pinhole. It felt like my body was being crushed by a ton of bricks.

His face contorted into a deranged toothy grin. "Ever heard of a whitewash?" he asked while smashing dirt and snow into my face and grinding them around.

I swore I felt rocks slicing my face into ribbons. I screamed, "Get off me, you fucking asshole!" loud enough to alert the neighbors within earshot. I used my voice like a rape whistle, shrieking the way only little girls and vixen foxes in heat can. It worked; they both got spooked and ran away as fast as they had appeared.

My first thought was, *Why doesn't he like me?* Then I thought, *Wait, does he like me?* I remembered the old saying, "If a boy is mean to you, it means he likes you." I'm paraphrasing, but you can catch my drift. I ran to the horrible daycare and went right up to the mirror to check for collateral damage. Surprisingly, my face was intact, and since there was no physical evidence of the attack, I didn't tell anyone. I couldn't muster the courage to be angry. Internalizing my shame was so much easier. Stuffing feelings down is always the best way to handle things, right?

I was overwhelmed with embarrassment that someone could hate me enough to do me harm, a feeling so contrary to my overall existence up to this point. Maybe I had brought it on myself for thinking redheads were cute? Banking this trauma enhanced a disproportionate fight-or-flight response, and Zelda, my inner red-eyed demon, was born. Like the birth of Aphrodite, who rose from the white foam produced by the severed genitals of Uranus, Zelda came into being from the white snow of whitewashing. The trauma at the hands of Steve O'Doyle, with my face plunged into the cold snow, became the trigger for my rage. If Audrina's voice was the angel on my shoulder, then Zelda's was the devil.

This particular incident made me understand how hard it must be for victims of rape, sexual assault, and domestic violence to come forward. Why are women expected to keep quiet and made to believe it's our fault? The sentiment that boys like you when they are mean to you primes little girls to accept abuse and programs the association of romance with violence and bad behavior. We have to stop spreading this misogynistic propaganda and stand up for one another. The age of feminism is long overdue. Let's empower our children to set boundaries, help them understand consent, say "stop" and "no," and listen to that feeling they get when danger is near. For the record, I still love redheads, but only the ones who respect my autonomy.

For my 10th birthday, Mom threw me a party at home with friends from the swim team and from the neighborhood. My Dad and LeeAnn, still in the dating phase, had called me earlier to let me know they would stop by to bring a present. When they arrived, they parked the car awkwardly outside of Mom's townhouse and asked a neighbor walking by to go in the house and tell me they were there.

I ran out of the house and jumped into the backseat, neglecting to tell Mom why I was leaving my own party. LeeAnn handed me a large, wrapped, oblong present. I tore it open to find a boombox in the most beautiful shade of cornflower blue. It was the perfect gift. I loved music and needed something to record all my favorite songs from the popular radio stations, which were always playing in our house and on car rides, including DC 101.1, Q107, WAVA 105.1, and WPGC-FM 95.5. The sound of music always seemed to make everyone happy. For me, music soothed the beast within me. It was a reminder of better times, and gave me the feeling of having a family back, the one I'd been trying so desperately to reunite or recreate.

Mom then came outside and made a beeline to Dad's driver's-side window. She was visibly distraught and asked why he hadn't coordinated the drop-off with her.

"We have guests!" she shrilled at him.

"We're only here for five minutes," Dad said. "I don't understand what the big deal is."

Mom scoffed and LeeAnn laughed. That made my mom lose her ever-loving shit. I thought, *Oh no, here comes Philly Kitty.*

"How about you step outside the car so we can discuss what's so funny?" she said, glaring at both of them.

LeeAnn rolled up her window and locked the door. I got out of the car with my new stereo in hand and said, "C'mon Mom, let's go back inside." Dad couldn't pull out of the parking lot fast enough. Happy birthday to me!

Part

II

"I want to be an 80s mom. Aw, they had it the best, didn't they? There used to be a commercial that came on at 10 o'clock at night that said, 'It's 10 p.m. Do you know where your children are?' They had to remind bitches they even had kids! Come on! Talk about the golden age of motherhood."

- CHRISTINA PAZSITSKY

CHAPTER THIRTEEN

UNFASHIONABLE

When my mom and I didn't get along, I felt like I'd lost my sounding board and best cheerleader. I also felt like I'd lost the love of my father and secretly hated and equally envied everyone with married parents. I had no empathy for Mom, who was trying to start over. I felt ashamed of our house, and I resented my parents for ending their marriage for their own benefit.

Without any warning or consultation, and soon after he married LeeAnn, we got a letter from Dad's attorney stating that Dad was limiting visitation from twice a week and every other weekend to once a month. Dad and LeeAnn would make sure to pick us up after dinner on Friday and have us back at Mom's right after breakfast on Sunday, which didn't even constitute a full weekend. Julie and I were heartbroken. Most parents fight each other in the courtroom to *gain* custody of their kids, but Dad was making it quite clear that he wanted to see less of us.

Being the queen of distractions, Mom got us into almost every sport and enrolled us in a month-long summer camp called Young Actors Theatre. My stage name was Gliss, and I wrote it everywhere, including in the wet cement for a new sidewalk in my neighborhood. I got my first real taste of show business and played exciting roles such as The Old Dog and Glinda the Good Witch of the North (with a Jersey accent) as well as less exciting roles such as Gopher and Kid 3. I learned about the intricacies of being on stage and how to be a part of a group that feeds off each other's energy. The most addicting part was the sound of laughter, which is possibly the reason I'm so enamored with female comedians today.

When things at home went wrong, I internalized my feelings and drew inward, like the time I was bullied for an eccentric outfit I wore to the first day of seventh grade at a new school, Langston Hughes Intermediate. Mom bought the outfit for me at Harvest Moon Company, the hippest local clothing store around. Years later, my sister got a job there. The owner avoided paying professionals to model his clothes by taking pictures of his staff wearing the clothes instead. They were all pretty girls from Reston, and their images were plastered all around the store and in the newspapers.

On one rare occasion, I was given free rein to choose a whole outfit. I chose a beige, hemp–cotton-blend turtleneck; a sage, satin cummerbund; and a long, green plaid, cotton muslin skirt. It all might have been a little too sophisticated for a 13-year-old. I looked more like a librarian from the late 1800s than a tween in the late 1980s. But I spent the whole morning sculpting my hair into a whimsical (a.k.a. lopsided) French twist to balance the look. I felt like a million bucks walking out the door and a badass walking all the way to school. Seventh graders didn't need a school bus; those were for children.

The minute I entered Langston Hughes, I noticed all the new faces giving me unfriendly up-and-down disgusted looks (otherwise known as "grit"), followed by eye rolls so hateful that they convinced me I was ugly. By second period, I was desperate to go home and change. Unfortunately, there were no do-overs for first-day attire. That stigma lasts a lifetime.

The seven years I spent cocooned at Terraset were now a distant memory. Five additional elementary schools had funneled into Langston Hughes, each with their own hierarchy of tormentors, unfamiliar fashion standards, and cultural protocols. I learned that clothes from the Gap and Britches meant you were preppy, department store clothes meant you were wealthy, and everything from K-mart was mocked relentlessly. Clothing from the Sunshine Surf Shop at Fair Oaks Mall was considered high fashion, and girls were expected to master the art of the bear claw, which required massive amounts of hairspray and a fine-tooth comb for teasing bangs into the shape of a crashing wave. It's probably the closest I'll ever get to actual surfing. The only acceptable lipstick colors were Silver City Pink or Frosted Brownie by Revlon, which was very unfortunate for someone with my olive complexion, Sun-In'd orange hair, and brown eyes. I never made the mistake of wearing my first-day-of-school clothes again. Just like my silk vest from Harrods in England, a gift from one of Mom's well-traveled friends, they stayed hanging in my closet for eternity.

Mom voiced her discontent for my sheep-like susceptibility to fads when I begged her to buy me an $80 Body Glove bikini, which is like $400 dollars now. It was barely 10 inches of fabric, but my best friend at the time, Danielle, had bought the same one and said it would look good on me. I cared way too much what others thought of me. I bitched about Mom's saggy size 10 aerobics leg warmer socks getting bunched up in the bottom of my shoes and was bitterly jealous of anyone who could afford their own socks, as well as starter jackets, parachute pants, and stone-washed jean jackets. Dad and LeeAnn, who was now my stepmom, bought me beautiful, coordinated outfits, but she allowed me to wear them only when I was staying with them on weekends. To me, that defeated the purpose of having nice clothes.

CHAPTER FOURTEEN

LIMNS OF THE LUDICROUS LATCHKEY

I was an inadequate latchkey kid, afflicted with a serious case of forgetfulness to locate and keep my keys. Even though they were attached to a rubber spiraled bracelet I was wearing, I lost my keys one day and, instead of facing the music, fabricated the most absurd and elaborate backstory.

I called the police from a neighbor's house and told them that I had fled the grasp of a pedophile who tried to lure me into his kidnapper van at the playground. I described a crazy-eyed, seven-foot tall, obese, White male wearing a kung fu mustache, aviator sunglasses, and suspenders who drove a white, windowless van. At some point during my fake near-abduction, I lost my keys, and that's why I was locked out of the house. I don't know where the lie came from, but once I got going with it, it snowballed. Still, I somehow managed to get away with it. The cops called my mom, who came home and let me back in the house. And for once, I didn't get grounded. I truly hope they never found the poor man that matched my ridiculous description.

Another incident that caused my summer to be cut short was the significant damage I caused by bringing all the neighborhood girls over to watch me power wash our kitchen floor with the outdoor hose. It seemed like a great idea, until all the terracotta-colored linoleum tiles began to warp and fold up around the corners. Water flooded into the living room, permeating the mustard-yellow shag carpet lying underneath our brass floor lamp, which left a permanent orange ring of rust on the yellow carpet. Our main level smelled like mold for over a year. I'm still waiting for the day when Mom and I can laugh about it together. Thank goodness I didn't hold my breath.

So in 1988, at age 12, I became the oldest camper at a daycare called Reston Children's Center and spent the summer performing unpaid grunt work. Like a shamash of the shul (Yiddish for "servant of the school"), I answered phones, printed, and collated papers. My first boss was a director named Ava Cook, who was from New Zealand. She took my mom's money along with my child labor and gave me the fancy title of "CIT": counselor-in-training.

In Hearthstone Court, we all judged our neighbor Maeve Morris for her public deflowering, meaning she talked about it openly; we didn't watch her have sex. We called her terms like "easy" or "loose," but all the virgins (like me) were secretly jealous. We wanted to know what it was like but didn't care to be slut-shamed like Maeve, whose reputation was sullied indefinitely. Yet the boy who took her virginity became cooler and more appealing for his "experience."

The pack of our neighborhood boys had built skate ramps to show off their skateboarding skills to all the young impressionable girls they wanted to seduce and desecrate, and, ipso facto, elevate themselves. After a week, the HOA forced them to demolish the ramps. Unlike the disappearing skate ramps, rumors followed Maeve all the way to high school, where she eventually failed out, or maybe she moved away; I can't remember. However, I took note of how harshly she was treated while the boys could do whatever they wanted. The more girls that a boy slept with, the more everyone admired him.

One night, before the forced removal, the boys sat perched on top of the most recently raised ramp, which was next to a small plot of land with trees and surrounded by a parking lot we called "the island." The girls and I lined up at the bottom, willingly subjecting ourselves to a game called "Good Looking or Good Personality?" We smiled like beauty pageant contestants and awaited the boys' judgment, which was doled out in a rating scale of 1 for ugly to 10 for perfect. Each body part received a score, starting with our feet, and each boy shouted out a number for every girl. They made their way up our bodies, ending with our hair.

Fortunately, I got a 10 in everything but my boobs. Unfortunately, my swollen nipple condition didn't count for real breasts. Luckily, the girls got a turn to judge the boys. We asked them to line up just as we had and shouted, "Take off your shirts. Payback's a bitch!" I believe this was the day multiple body complexes and dysmorphic syndromes were born all around. I still find it hard to fathom that I voluntarily exposed myself to such harsh scrutiny and, in turn, directed it toward others as well.

Back at Langston Hughes, I met Lorena, the most dangerous girl in our class and the Svengali of concert choir, on the first day of seventh grade. Her well-established network of friends from the Swaying Woods neighborhood smoked cigarettes, skipped school, and wore copious amounts of dark eyeliner and baggy clothes. Lorena's violent temper secured her spot as the class alpha female. Everyone was either desperate to be her friend or scared shitless of her, but I chose to make her my ally.

Lorena and I connected instantly and became the closest of friends. We started a piercing business for the choir, and whenever the teacher left the room, we'd take a lighter to a safety pin (for sanitary purposes), stab a brave customer's earlobe, and close the pin so they could wear it like a new earring. By the end of first quarter, everyone was sporting an "in-between seamstress alteration" look.

One day in the cafeteria, we spotted a new girl named Danielle sitting with the school nerds and decided to approach her. "Hey!" Lorena spoke first.

"Where are you from?" I asked.

"Long Island, New York," she replied shyly.

"That's cool. Do you want to come sit with us and tell us about it?" The look of relief on her face was unmistakable.

Recruiting new members to the tribe was my favorite pastime and great foreshadowing for my future career. Danielle and I stayed friends through college, and that small act of kindness went a long way. I'd like to think that bit of good will brought me some good karma when I needed it later on.

Well into our seventh-grade year, Lorena and I were walking along a path with a couple of her groupies and spotted a fellow choir member, Rebecca Morose, who was walking in the opposite direction. For some crazy, unknown reason, Lorena skewered a dog turd with a stick and started waving it around Rebecca's face, demanding she eat it. Rebecca stepped back, tripped over a root, and fell to the ground. Lorena was merciless and hit Rebecca on her cheek with the poop stick. I quickly grabbed it out of her hand and threw it as far as I could, like a literal baton toss, to protect the underdog. My defensive instincts were in full force.

Rebecca got up and took off into a sprint through the woods. I turned to Lorena and yelled, "What the hell are you doing?! That was not cool and was super fucking disgusting!" I didn't know what had come over her, but I knew that nothing about it was right. She instantly transferred her fury from Rebecca to me, and because I was outnumbered, I decided to run as well. Lorena and her groupies chased me until they realized where I was headed, up the giant, 58-degree hill to my townhouse.

The next day at school, I felt like I had a target on my back. Lorena had spread vicious lies about me, saying I'd made disparaging remarks about her sister's medical condition. I told everyone, including her sister, that Lorena had made it up, but in seventh grade the truth is never as interesting. Lorena's scorn was the real crowd-pleaser, and her entourage of sycophants taunted me incessantly.

Lorena found me in a hallway right in front of my classroom. I braced myself for a screaming match. Instead, she charged at me, screaming, "YOU are a FUCKING BITCH!" and slapped me across the face with enough force to send me reeling. The pain was sharp, tears welled up in my eyes, and my nose started to run involuntarily. I just stood there, bewildered and paralyzed with fear. I cried silently while the realization that I was no longer safe at school crept over me like a spider infestation.

My impotence in this moment haunts me to this very day. For years, I'd lie awake at night replaying on a loop the mental anguish and shame of getting slapped by Lorena. Even when I did sleep, my dreams were perforated with the same recurring nightmare: my limbs turned to stone, and my tongue became a spongy, cotton-like, choking mass, inhibiting my ability to run away, scream, and breathe. Then I'd wake up fighting for breath and holler a strangled "Ahhhh!," waking everyone in the house and, later, my college dorm.

When I told my mom what happened, she told me an inspirational story about how she'd saved a little girl at school from getting her lunch money robbed by a bunch of big bullies. In Mom's story, she offered to bring the bullies lunch so they didn't have to steal from the little girl, and they responded with threats, demanding she meet them outside. This was South Philadelphia in the 1960s.

The bullies were already In the school yard with at least 10 of their friends when Mom arrived. They all started laughing when Mom realized she couldn't get back inside the cafeteria—someone had locked the doors behind her—so she remained at the top of the steps with her back against the door. The biggest girl said, "Get off the stairs," and Mom replied, "No, thanks. You can come and get me."

Mom waited until they were one step below her, then placed her foot right between the big bully's giant boobs and kicked so hard that the girl flew down the stairs and landed on a couple of the other girls behind her. One got her arm caught between the side railing spokes. Some of the girls went to help the injured, but the rest continued to advance on my mom. She heard them saying things like, "Rip her clothes off" and "Get her by the hair," and she began punching and scratching, keeping her feet kicking. There was no one in authority around to stop the fight. She was sure if she stopped punching and kicking someone would actually knock her down, and if they were successful she may never get back up.

Suddenly, they all backed away and someone grabbed Mom from behind and pulled her into the cafeteria. She never got to see the carnage, but she heard the sirens of ambulances that showed up. The big girl had broken her arm, the girl whose arm was caught in the railing had dislocated her shoulder, and another girl had broken her leg when the big girl fell on top of her. Mom knew she'd landed a great many punches, and she had skin under all her fingernails, but she didn't have a scratch on her and her clothes were all intact.

My mom's story made me realize that if she could defend herself against 10 bullies, surely I could defend myself against one! However, my childhood belief that I could always find the helpers, as Mr. Rogers had promised, died that day. My innocence and naivete took their leave as well and were replaced by a dark force. Lorena was the last girl to ever hit me in the face.

The understanding that all people aren't inherently good and we're not always safe in school is a basic part of growing up. After learning more about Lorena's disturbing homelife—it was rumored that her father had committed suicide and her mother, who was left alone with six kids, a mortgage, and a store to run, stole money from her children's friends—I began to think that maybe Lorena was a product of her environment. I don't know what happened to her specifically, but no one is born that evil. In a very hard way, I had to learn the lesson that we can all fall victim to weakness.

CHAPTER FIFTEEN

THE DEXTER BULLY

I kept Lorena at arms' length, knowing I'd never really be her friend again, despite the multiple attempts she made to reconcile.

"Let's skip third and go over to Brandi's," she once suggested. "Christian just scored some acid."

"No, thanks. I've got a test today," I replied, still valuing my sanity and the location of all my serotonin.

She was the same old sociopath from her poop-stick-wielding days, and I'd heard through the grapevine she'd landed herself in hot water legally for similar offenses, but I wasn't scared of her anymore. I now had leverage. My mom's threats to file charges must have frightened her off.

Lorena moved onto weaker victims, like Tabitha Tucker, a frail blonde with pale-gray eyes framed in tortoise-rimmed glasses who was ripe for Lorena's wrath. At the height of Lorena and Tabitha's dissension, I saw Tabitha pulling books out of her locker in a panic. A crowd had formed in the locker commons behind Lorena, who was moving toward us with the same battle-starved glare from the slap incident and the same army of Swaying Woods ilk following behind her like hungry wolves. We were sandwiched between the six-foot-tall rows of locker commons on either side. This was the location of daily ass beatings where, to be saved, one must hoist themselves on top of the lockers, locate the nucleus of the conflict, then jump down into the chaos. Since most administrators never saw who did what (in other words, weren't brave enough to scale the lockers and break up a fight between twelve- and thirteen-year-olds), everyone got in trouble, even the sorry sap getting beaten up.

Everyone squeezed together, blocking our exit from the aisle. I grabbed Tabitha's hand and ran in the opposite direction, pushing through the other nosy assemblage toward the back of the school. I tugged her down a curved hall to cut off the mob's line of sight. I never let go of her hand and dragged her into a random classroom halfway down the building's east end, where we hid until the bell rang. Who knows what would have happened if I hadn't taken Tabitha by the hand and dragged her to a safe location. I just knew that I had to do it. I had to stand up for someone who couldn't stand up for herself. The karmic wheel of fighting for the underdog kept circling.

Later, I was saved by two tall, beautiful, tough girls, both named Tanya, from getting beat up by a girl twice my size—another one of Lorena's pawns. I called them the "Tough Tanyas." I met one of them a year prior on the first day of seventh grade in Mrs. Masako's social studies class. I overheard her say, "I hate all White people."

I was sitting right next to her, and my heart skipped a beat in anticipation. I challenged, "Wait. Does that mean you hate me?"

She said, "Well, you're White, so yes."

This was before my tanning salon addiction, but I made it my plight to become her friend. Clearly, her readiness to take a hit for me proved that my efforts weren't in vain, and I'm still grateful after all these years.

The constant fighting was like a merry-go-round of harassment, adrenaline, violence, and shame, over and over again. The flip side was that boys started to finally notice me around sixth grade. Some wanted to "go out," which meant talking on the phone, eating lunch together, and holding hands. Despite being boy crazy since kindergarten, I didn't have the faintest idea of what romance or love was. So after enough teasing, such as, "Ellen and [fill in the blank] sitting in a tree, K.I.S.S.I.N.G.," I'd get antsy. And when the connection between that boy and I wore off, I recognized dating to be a game of power. I did the dumping to avoid getting dumped. Who knows where I'd land? Eventually, the technique backfired. In seventh grade, I ended a relationship with a boy named Chris Tinkle because the novelty had worn off. I hoped we could stay friends and treat our brief time together like the rite of passage it was, but Chris was deeply injured by the offense and wanted retribution in the form of blood.

The summer I turned 13, I invited my Glade swim teammates Stacey, Erin, and Jenn over to my house after practice to experiment with my mom's basement liquor cabinet. At the time, these girls were my closest friends, and we did everything together. Also, in our age group we had a killer relay team. Jenn had the best backstroke, Erin had the best freestyle, Stacey's forte was the breaststroke, and mine was the butterfly. Erin was obsessed with U2 and had a crush on a boy named Derrick, whose eyes resembled the same pattern of starburst furrows in his irises as Bono's. Derrick happened to be Chris's friend. I was completely unaware of how much I had wounded Chris by breaking up with him earlier and dismissed the troublesome warning signs. I also fancied myself a matchmaker and decided to invite the boys to booze it up with us.

We swiped a bottle of Peach Schnapps and another liquor that had a very strange taste. It was called Galliano and came in a long, skinny, yellow bottle. We went out to the patio to enjoy the sunny day. After finishing both bottles, I went inside to find more liquor.

Unbeknownst to me, Chris had brought spray paint to execute a premeditated plan, fueled by revenge and liquid courage: to decorate my neighbor's fence and our concrete patio by spelling out "I LOVE ELLEN" in giant black letters on both. He chucked the evidence into the woods and cowardly ran home before I came back.

Later that night, our neighbor Mr. Wojtowicz darkened our doorstep, holding the can of spray paint he found in the woods and reporting music so loud it shook his house. I was called a myriad of hurtful names, and Mom forced me to use my allowance to purchase paint thinner and to write and hand-deliver a letter of apology to him. The next day I spent hours removing the vandalism from the patio and fence.

When we returned to Langston Hughes in the fall, I saw Chris in my English class with our teacher, Mr. Butterfield, and sighed. The beef between us escalated at lunch. He was muttering passive-aggressive comments under his breath every time I said something. When I got up to throw away my food, I bumped into him, causing him to drop something onto his shirt. I said, "Oops! I'm sorry" and smirked. It felt good to give him a dose of his own medicine. He picked up a french fry, drenched it in ketchup, and threw it at me. I ducked and threw back a fry dunked in chocolate ice cream. Then the whole table joined in and screamed, "Food fight!" Everyone was laughing except for Chris and me. We were at war.

When the lunch monitors resumed control, I grabbed the rectangular shaped slice of pizza and snuck out through the cafeteria doors. I took a concealed position behind a column out in the open space, careful to stay clear of the deadly labyrinth of aisles. I readied myself as Chris walked by looking relaxed and happy. I grabbed the back of his head, seized a handful of his unwashed red hair in my fist, and smashed the pizza into his face as hard as I could, sliding it upward a bit to ensure the contents made it into his nostrils. Then I ran as fast as I could to my least favorite class (math) and sat in the back corner to hide and catch my breath.

A couple of kids streamed in behind me to find out what the hell was going on. I was telling the story when Mr. Pizza Face stormed into the room and lurched at me. He knocked me off the desk and onto the ground. I wrestled to get up but was stuck underneath the weight of his body. With his hands clutched around my neck, I dug my nails into his face. I tried to kick him off and was twisting his hands with mine to squirm free of his iron grip. As Ted Nugent's lyrics echoed in my ears, "I got you in a stranglehold baby /That night I crushed your face"), the lights started to fade in the periphery of my sight. Where was Zelda when I needed her? I would have lost consciousness if it wasn't for my friend Mack Laramey who came to my rescue. Mack was my hero that day.

Mack's soft-spoken voice was so low it had a buzzing quality. He was tall, very dark, handsome, and painfully thin, but he was strong enough to pull Chris off me, which was more than anyone else did, including the teacher. Chris and I were both sent to the principal's office and suspended. Suspension didn't seem all that bad when I could have died at the hands of Chris.

Upon our return from suspension, Mr. Butterfield sat us down and forced Chris and me to talk it out. I faked remorse and fought the urge to smile at the four parallel scabs raised along Chris's left cheek. I appreciated Mr. Butterfield's attempts to make things right. Transitioning from Terraset to Langston Hughes had been like going from summer camp to a gen pop prison; I was just another number, a useless face in the crowd of five amalgamated schools. I longed for the security of having teachers who were genuinely interested in their student's' well-being. No one except Mr. Butterfield blinked an eye over the assault. I'd love to blame it on a lack of resources, but that wasn't the case. The resources were there, but no one seemed interested enough in using them.

In addition to those I had with Steve, Lorena, and Chris, I eventually engaged in 22 proper fights during my youth, but not all of them were for such noble reasons as saving someone else from getting their ass kicked. I like to tell people I'm a bully tormentor, or a bully of bullies—just like Dexter was a serial killer of serial killers—but I was never a bully. I was jumped twice, once by three girls from rival Herndon High School and once by four senior cheerleaders when I was a junior. Nonetheless, I was resolute in ensuring that I did not take any hits to the face or receive any slaps while engaged in the fight.

I take pride in the fights where I was defending those who couldn't stand up for themselves, like Tabitha. I knew what it was like to feel paralyzed by fear and shame, and I never wanted anyone else to experience that. I was inspired by my mom and my neighbor Bahija, who always tried to protect me.

CHAPTER SIXTEEN

BAHIJA

I met Bahija when we moved to Hearthstone Court in 1984. She was two years older than me and lived just four doors down. Her first experience with Terraset was very different from my own. On Bahija's first day of kindergarten, her grandmother escorted her to the classroom. The teacher bent down to look Bahija in the eyes and spoke to her like she was hard of hearing.

"Hello, how are you?" she asked.

Bahija mimicked her strange inflection and replied, "I'm fine, how are you?"

Her grandmother nudged Bahija, who looked up at her and shrugged, assuming the teacher was born with some kind of intellectual handicap.

After her grandmother left, an adorable White boy with icy blue eyes walked up to Bahija, grabbed her hand, and bent her fingers backward. She winced in pain and wriggled free, but not before he spit in her face, called her the n-word, and then walked away. The whole class, including the teacher, saw it happen and did nothing.

The remainder of Bahija's elementary school career was fraught with violence. She ate lunch and spent recess hiding in the bathroom. It wasn't until sixth grade that she started to stand up for herself and make friends.

The fluorescent lights in Bahija's kitchen were always on, but there was a big plant blocking the window, so I could never see inside. I was never invited in and, somehow, had enough sense not to ask why. So we hung out outside a lot. Even after dark, we forfeited primetime television for games of flashlight tag. We stepped foot inside only to seek shelter from a storm or to raid my kitchen when we were absolutely starving.

Our family's kitchen food supply was barely sufficient for Mom, Jules, and me. The refrigerator was poorly equipped with a mixture of condiments and disparate items, including horseradish, bagels, and spoiled sun-dried tomato pasta, leading to an unpleasant realization that such food combinations could induce food poisoning akin to shellfish. This experience underscored the importance of us promptly disposing of leftovers within four days. Dinners were usually ramen noodles with an egg, "For protein!" Mom would say, or something frozen, like a Lean Cuisine meal or chicken cordon bleu from Price Club, the precursor to Costco. Mom still calls it Price Club.

During the holidays, Mom kept bowls of assorted nuts scattered around the house. We were watching TV one night when I cracked open a Brazil nut. After biting into it, I felt something moving inside and glanced down at the half I was still holding to find a translucent, half-eaten maggot. I spit out what I was chewing in horror.

"Oh, my God!" I shrieked.

"Looks like you got a bad nut," Mom said. "Don't worry, it's just a little protein."

I didn't know how to cook because I wasn't interested in learning anything from Mom. Our personalities were so similarly stubborn, with only a nanometer-sized fuse, that we clashed like bulls, even though we're both Leos. Our birthdays are only eight days apart. Julie's a Leo too, which made our house a feline war zone once a month from a phenomenon known as the "dormitory effect."

Julie avoided the fire with constant optimism. She followed Mom around like a thirsty kitten. By doing so, she went from amateur sous chef to gourmet cook in a week. She incorporated the same technique with teachers and coaches, earning superlatives on the swim team such as "Coach's Shadow." Eventually, when she was only 10 years old and I was only 13, Julie taught me how to turn on the stove, boil water, and use the toaster and microwave. Before that, Bahija and I were on our own after school, raiding the fridge and consuming whatever was remotely edible. It was Bahija who taught me how to "scrap cook," meaning doing what we could with what you could find. We'd make peanut butter and jelly sandwiches—sometimes without peanut butter, sometimes without jelly, sometimes without bread. But we made it work. She once pieced together a meal by squeezing mustard onto a bologna slice and rolling it up, saying, "Voilà! A burrito." She added, "Hotdogs don't need to be cooked or even microwaved because they're basically the same thing as bologna." I don't know whether that was true or necessarily good for my tummy, but they tasted exactly the same to me.

Bahija and I were two peas in a pod. We sang Madonna's "La Isla Bonita" in perfect harmony, learned all 17 tracks on RUN DMC's *Raising Hell* album, gossiped about the other girls we knew, and told each other about our crushes. We also put on plays for the whole neighborhood. I was the creator of content and the recruiter of actors (our little sisters and their friends), and Bahija was the director. I wrote myself into the starring role, as the devil, which left Julie the supporting actress role—angel, of course.

My days with Bahija were spent trying to crack each other up. Her laughter resembled a hiccup, yet with such an endearing honking quality that it became my favorite sound, akin to winning a prize every time I heard it. Our time together was a distraction from our problems, at school, at home, and with our parents. Bahija and I had the same goal: to make each other happy when we were feeling sad or insecure.

During one sleepover, we took my mom's hidden liquor from the shelf in my dank, cement basement laundry room. We drank enough to feel tipsy and then fell asleep on the pull-out couch while watching a movie. Bahija insisted that the TV should stay on throughout the night. In the morning, we realized the alcohol had backfired. Bahija woke up to find that she had gotten sick on her pillow while sleeping. At the time, we thought sleep vomiting was hilarious. However, we now know that doing strange things in her sleep was a symptom of a trauma that would haunt Bahija throughout her adolescence and young adulthood. Maybe that's why we gravitated toward each other in earnest. Bahija was suffering in her own way, and I was acting out as a way to get attention for all the things I lacked on the home front.

I don't know why Bahija loved me; she had so many demons of her own to fight. Unlike in elementary school, she grew to be strong in her adolescence. She fought as an advocate for herself and for those around her, especially the underdogs like me. I was an awkward, troubled girl with the unfortunate combination of knock-knees and pigeon toes. Luckily, Bahija knew some tricks to fix my awkward gait and showed me how to walk in a straight line with my feet turned out. "Walk like a ballerina prepared to plié at any given moment," she'd say. The technique worked.

She, along with Zach Thorton, my first love and the king of Hearthstone Court, also taught me how to fight by aiming past the target (follow through), stun punching with my left and power punching with my right (a combo), and holding my fingers in a fist so I didn't break my thumb. She told me I was beautiful when I was at my ugliest. She was my champion, my mentor, and the older sister replacement for my cousin Shannon, who had been forced to abandon me by her mother over a family dispute that lasted decades. Shannon, once the person I was happiest to see, was now a ghost from a happier time.

Bahija was already in South Lakes High School while I was still at Langston Hughes Intermediate. The schools were next to each other, so we would walk together. But she would always drop me off safely at Langston Hughes before backtracking to go to the high school. When I asked her why she went so far out of the way, she said, "Because I don't want you to get beat up." I loved her fiercely in return. She also cared about me when no one else did.

One of the Hearthstone boys had set up a hemp, macramé hammock between two trees in the woods behind our neighborhood, the strings tied together with a wooden rod on either side. I was sitting on one, alongside five other kids, really enjoying the inclusion, when Marc Glass decided to chop the hammock down with a machete. My (back then) skinny ass dropped six feet and landed with a loud thud. The wooden rod was perfectly situated between my butt cheeks, directly under my coccyx, and the force of the fall broke my tailbone. I tried to hide the reflexive tears streaming down my face because I couldn't bear the added humiliation of crying in front of a bunch of cool kids after breaking such an embarrassing area of my body. I climbed up the hill and slumped over, careful not to turn around to let them see my face covered in anguish and shame. It was excruciatingly painful to walk. Marc and the other boys were laughing. No one seemed to care, and no one followed me. Except Bahija.

CHAPTER SEVENTEEN

THE DYSLEXIC POOL-HOPPER

Close to the end of eighth grade and my time at Langston Hughes, my grades were slipping, and it wasn't just because I was being bullied. According to my mother and teachers, my IQ was too high for me to be performing so poorly, which is indicative of a learning disability. Also, the lack of routine and stability at home started to bleed over into my schoolwork. I was unorganized and easily distracted, and I couldn't catch up. I talked often in class and was labeled a troublemaker.

The American Psychiatric Association began to recognize ADHD in the late 1980s, but recognition of the disorder was slow to progress in schools. Luckily for me, a clinical neuropsychologist who was trained and experienced in the assessment of learning disabilities arrived at Langston Hughes. She referred me for testing, and I was diagnosed with ADHD and slight dyslexia by the end of that school year. This was great news! I'd always assumed I was just an idiot, a word I couldn't even spell. Other impossible words to spell include "exercise," "diarrhea," and "vacuum," and I just had to look up and spell check all three words before writing them down.

Mom sent me to a tutor named Nora Buchanon, who welcomed me into her home twice a week to practice math. She kept her fridge stocked with exotic things such as white grape juice and mint jelly, and she let me try new things each visit. I tried to pay attention to her instruction, but it was no use. I barely had a nodding relationship with math and don't remember one single concept of algebra. However, I remember every kindness from Nora Buchannon. The flavor of white grape juice and mint jelly still tastes like sympathy and compassion to me.

To this day, I have to Google how to convert numbers into percentages and use basic arithmetic to put myself to sleep at night. My brain gets tired from all the possibilities and thinking. The treatment was an individualized education plan, which included a special class called "Basic Skills Resources" for one whole period with a designated teacher who allowed untimed tests and extra time to complete homework. I disparagingly referred to it as my LD (learning disability) class. I was also given a prescription for Ritalin, which has since been substituted by Adderall (dextroamphetamine). Ritalin works by increasing the amount of dopamine released in an area of the brain related to motivation, action, and cognition, which helped me perform better in school. I paid more attention to my teachers and took copious legible notes.

Unfortunately, the positive effects of Ritalin were ephemeral and usurped by the lengthier repercussions of the comedown, which aided my intolerance for side eyes and running mouths. Most of my fights and subsequent suspensions were a direct result of my meds wearing off, not to mention my off-the-charts insomnia that added catastrophic chaos to my already disorganized mornings. No wonder I couldn't find my keys! I stopped taking the pills and started selling them for $5 each. Mom wasn't the only one who knew how to hustle.

My birthday party that summer was a sleepover for me and my closest friends. We were too old to play the greatest hits from my childhood, such as Light as a Feather, Stiff as a Board, a game requiring only two fingers to lift one of us high above our heads, or Bloody Mary, where we'd turn off the lights, light a candle, say her name, and spin around three times to try to resurrect her bloody image in the bathroom mirror. We couldn't find the Ouija board to contact my Aunt Caroline, so I choreographed a fantastic dance routine to "Situation" by Yazoo instead. I summoned my mom to watch the finished product and take pictures. "Wow! Fantastic moves, darling!" she cheered.

Around midnight, we snuck out through the basement's sliding glass doors to go pool-hopping. We walked along the path using the silver light of the moon and climbed the fence at Glade Pool for a little dip with some boys who just happened to be doing the very same thing at the very same time. Pool-hopping was a popular pastime for lawbreaking teens who didn't concern themselves with simple, class-one misdemeanors like trespassing.

We snuck back inside the same way we left, through the basement's sliding glass doors. But this time, around 2 a.m., my mom was sitting on the couch waiting for us. She fumed as she packed everyone into 'Ken,' the name given to our car to pay tribute to our kind neighbor Kenny Marshall, delighted to discover his name and birthday coincidentally on the license plate. Mom then chauffeured each of my friends to their homes, where each parent answered the door sluggishly and slightly annoyed. Mom told the sleepy-eyed parents, "These girls snuck out of my house to go to the pool and didn't come home till two a.m. Call me in the morning with any questions." Not one of the half-dozen girls who attended my party were allowed to come to my house or hang out with me outside of school ever again. My family of friends (my "fr-amily") disappeared as quickly as my real nuclear one had. So, I made new ones.

My friend Carolyn Bergstein's dad had full custody of her in middle school, which was rare at that time. This was also when time with my own dad began to dwindle due to the birth of my brother Brandon, Dad and LeeAnn's son. I was so excited when he was born; I couldn't wait for him to grow up and be my new best friend. I told everyone who would listen that I had a new baby brother. But then months went by without an invitation to visit. I didn't know it at the time, but LeeAnn was going through postpartum depression—just like my mom had. I was incredibly jealous of Carolyn and all the time she got to be with her dad, but I soon discovered that the grass isn't always greener.

During one sleepover, Carolyn and I snuck out to meet up with friends on top of the pyramid that poked through the lawn covering the roof of Terraset Elementary, which was right across the street from Carolyn's house. We drank her dad's stash of Bartles and James wine coolers and then went home to make up songs about the fridge full of vegetables resembling deformed penises.

"How did you convince your dad to let us have the house for the night?" I asked.

"I just told him we'd behave and take care of ourselves with a tone of great authority," she replied.

"I wish that worked with my parents," I said solemnly, but in my head I knew she'd been abandoned for the weekend.

Once, Carolyn and I shoplifted Rit Dye and plain T-shirts from Woolworth's department store inside Fair Oaks Mall so we could go home and make tie-dye shirts. Carolyn stuffed the Fruit of the Loom shirts under her bra and waistline of her pants, and I put the Rit Dye in my pocket. We never made it home with the goods. A security guard spotted us in the convex mirrors hanging from the ceiling, intercepted us on our way through the back entrance to Burger

King, and called the police. We were given a court date to appear before a judge to receive our punishment. To make matters worse, the incident's court date interfered with a previously scheduled (and paid for by Mom) sleep-away camp at Camp Louise.

Camp Louise was for Jewish girls and the only place I'd ever been, other than a synagogue, where my Judaic heritage didn't lump me into the minority. Julie and I wrote home every day. Her letters were short: "Please send more snacks. I miss you. Love, Julie Beth." Mine were much longer, riddled with spelling and grammatical mistakes, and spilled the beans about each girl in my bunk.

Getting dropped into the woods with a bunch of strangers was intimidating at first, but once we sat down for our first meal in the cafeteria, to my amazement, everyone started singing the Hamotzi Prayer Song: "Our voices rise in song together, as our joyful prayer is said. Baruch ata Adonai, Eloheinu Melech ha-olam, hamotzi lechem min ha'aretz, Amen" We sang in unison. It's one of the few Hebrew prayers I already knew from my dad, who made us recite it every night before a meal. I felt like I belonged.

One day, like a pack of Jewish angels, we all wore white clothing and learned how to perform sign language to the song "Stand by Me." My bunk leader used Aussie shampoo and hairspray to tame her curly blonde hair, which made our whole bunk smell like peach bubblegum. On the last night, we met the boys from Camp Airy, Camp Louise's brother camp, where the cutest boy named Jake asked me to dance. It felt like I had finally found my people and was starring in my very own rom-com.

I was having the time of my life, but unfortunately my former criminal activity forced me to leave early for a court ordered appearance. I didn't tell anyone, even the ones I knew I could trust. I felt like Camp Lousie was a start-over for me. No one there knew about any of the trouble I was constantly getting into back home. Camp Louise was my tabula rasa (blank slate), a chance to get my innocence back by exhibiting socially acceptable behavior. All it took was a change of environment, but unfortunately I had to go home to face the music on my court date. And after getting caught shoplifting at a store that everyone made fun of for being a place where only grandmothers shopped, I decided to step up my stealing game instead of standing down.

For a while, Julie and I were the same exact size, barely an A cup, but she gained on me fast. Her employment at the most popular clothing store in town helped her curate the most beautiful new wardrobe. Every morning before jumping into the shower, she'd lay out an outfit on her bed. One day, I waited until the water was running and put on every single garment, including the underwear, then pretended as though she'd purposefully laid all the clothes out for me. She did not appreciate the misappropriation of her prudent preparation and chased me around the house threatening to stab me with a fork.

I tried on a bathing suit during one of Julie's shifts, a blue one-piece that said *La Mer*, French for "the sea." I put on my clothes over it and walked out of the dressing room and out the front door. Once I knew Jules could be trusted not to rat me out, I convinced her to set our sights on a more sophisticated operation.

Christmas was approaching, and the concept of gifting our parents with items from a store, or anything of monetary value, was foreign to us. We went to Macy's and entered the fitting rooms as A cups, and we left as solid double Ds., smuggling as many wired, padded bras as we could. And we didn't stop at bras. I took a small, engraved glass jewelry box with a mirrored bottom for Mom, rhinestone necklaces and two pairs of earrings for me, a tennis bracelet for LeeAnn, and dress socks for Dad.

When Mom opened her gifts, Jules and I said, "Dad gave us money for presents." We said the reverse when Dad opened his gifts.

The heist remained our best kept secret, since each parent refused to communicate or acknowledge the other.

I don't know what compelled me to steal. "Compelled" is a word that always reminds me of *The Exorcist* and a scary-as-shit little girl named Regan who says, "You're gonna to die up there," then pees on the rug in front of all her mom's coworkers surrounding the piano at her mom's drunken holiday party. Talk about not being in control of your own body! I think I stole because of my deep need for control over my new sense of self. I was hyper-aware of the image associated with our demoted socioeconomic status, and I didn't like it one bit. Maybe it was a need for attention, or maybe I just liked taking risks and getting away with some kind of reward. Maybe I wanted to make people happy and bring people together, to replace my former nuclear family. It was probably a little bit of all those things, but I was headed down a dark road, and I wasn't even in high school yet.

CHAPTER EIGHTEEN

THE CAVEWOMAN ISN'T A RAT

I entered South Lakes High School already a delinquent teen. Shoplifting, drinking, and smoking were all norms in my little world, and I was a magnet for seeking out others who were like me. Anyone who made me feel normal, no matter what trouble they were causing, was good for me. I wanted, I needed, to be in the thick of it all.

When I first moved to Hearthstone Court, I felt the need to prove myself. My next-door neighbor, Ada Wojtowicz, and I had matching sweaters; mine was red and hers was blue. On Freaky Friday I went to the bus stop, pretending to be Ada. I wore my red sweater and a pair of fake glasses and imitated her higher-pitched speaking voice. I started to get a reaction from the crowd, which Ada did not care for, and she began to cry. I took the glasses off and told her that imitation was the best form of flattery and promised I'd halt the production and find another way to get points with our teacher. I turned all my clothes inside out and won the Freaky Friday contest.

Ada forgave me, and we kept unintentionally dressing alike, including homecoming dance dresses of metallic gold and black satin. But making fun of this sweet, adorable, impeccably well-behaved girl next door haunts me to this very day.

Ada's mother volunteered for everything, just like my mom had done before the divorce, making me more resentful of the multiple jobs and other people that stole all of Mom's time and energy. I was also jealous of my next-door neighbors because they lived with their dad.

In ninth grade, Mrs. Wojtowicz chaperoned our choir for an 18-hour field trip bus ride to Chicago's Six Flags. It would be the first time I tried dip, curious to see what all the fuss was about. Just like when I was in elementary school, I needed to fit in. All the boys at Hearthstone Court liked Skoal Bandits in wintergreen or Copenhagen pouches and carried around disgusting, brown saliva-filled water bottles. The tobacco felt like it burned a hole in my mouth. I could handle it for only 30 seconds, tops. At first it tasted sweet and slightly minty, but once the chemical component kicked in, I became dizzy and then nauseous. I ran to the back of the bus and threw up in the repulsive bathroom.

My affluent friend Bethy had parents who were also divorced, and she too had little supervision at home. One school night, she picked me up in a red sedan to go to a party with a kid named Alex Jackson, who was in the driver's seat. I knew of him but had never met him in person before. The party became lively as a group of 20 young men congregated in the basement. I felt a little out of my element in that setting, but as we indulged in Milwaukee's best beer (affectionately dubbed "Beast"), smoked Marlboro Light cigarettes, and played cards, the calming effects of alcohol soon made me feel more at ease. My curfew approached, but Bethy and Alex weren't ready to go, so Alex tossed the keys to my new classmate Brett and told him to drive me and my buddy Sam Georgopolis home.

On Sunrise Valley Drive, just before the turn onto the road that led to my house, sirens and lights flashed behind us. Brett started to melt down. He pulled into a neighborhood, nervously drove all the way into the cul-de-sac at the bottom, and yelled, "I don't even have my license yet!" Sam and I tried to calm him down, but once the car stopped he put it in park, frantically hopped out, and ran into the woods behind the houses. Two cops chased him on foot.

Sam and I looked at each other, our eyes wide and afraid. We contemplated running too but decided to stay put. "We didn't do anything wrong," I reasoned.

The cops returned holding Brett's hands behind his back and slammed his head on the hood of the car before handcuffing him. All three of us were placed in the back of the cop's car.

"Don't be a rat," Sam instructed, although I had no idea what kind of incriminating dirt I could have possibly possessed.

When we got to the station, the cops separated us into three interrogation rooms and handed me a binder full of suspect mug-shots. They asked me to identify Alex, whom I spotted plain as day, sporting the same exact Kid and Play high-top fade from when he'd picked me up earlier in the evening. This was the moment I finally understood the severity of the situation. The vehicle we were caught driving was a stolen car!

I did what I was told and kept my mouth shut, simulating igno-rance until they told me I could go home. I knew once my mom found out, I would be grounded for a month, or worse. This could be the tipping point for military school, which my mom had been threatening to send me to for over a year. I begged the cops not to call my mother, making the case that I didn't know the car was sto-len and she'd murder me if she had to pick me up from the police station. They obliged and drove me home themselves, but I became crestfallen the moment I realized they intended to escort me all the way to my front door.

As my mom opened the door, I observed the color slowly fading from her face. I was supposed to be studying at Bethy's house. As the police informed her of my involvement in stealing a car, I witnessed the color rushing back into her cheeks in a wave of anger. My legs turned to jelly, and I could hear my own heartbeat in my ears. The cops added fuel to the fire by saying, "Your daughter insisted she'd be in harm's way if we called you. Do we need to be concerned?" I felt a churning sensation inside my stomach and envisioned a fish flopping around inside, yearning for release back into the water.

Mom's smile was ear to ear but stopped short of her eyes. She assured the officers that I would live to see another day and thanked them for bringing me home. She closed the door behind the officers as they left, then turned to me, no longer smiling. I was grounded for a month. I wouldn't be allowed to participate in the talent show, the one where I'd choreographed a dance routine to "Iko Iko" for me and six other girls. Those girls went on to perform the routine in front of the whole school while I sat and watched from the bleachers. Dancing was so joyous for me, and I'd been counting down the days until the show. Mom knew taking that away from me would hurt me most. Nothing felt fair.

Everyone I cared about seemed to turn on me, including the girls from the pool-hopping party, my friends from the talent show, and a boy I'd been dating who suddenly cheated on me with my best friend Stacey from the swim team. This betrayal, coupled with my parents' divorce, planted within me a lasting skepticism toward others. I already had a reputation for being a fighter and seemed to attract other fighters into my sphere. One afternoon, a girl I'd never even met before named Pamela started a fight with me for what seemed like no apparent reason. Maybe she thought I was an easy target. I realized she wanted to beat me up when she followed me to the locker commons, threatening me with insults. My inner demon Zelda appeared in an instant. Zelda had zero patience for words and turned around to face Pamela. Dropping my shoulders to release my heavy backpack to the ground, I said, "Let's go!" and waited for Pamela to hit first.

Like a caged animal, Zelda was set free and used everything she had to prevent us from getting pinned. We kicked so hard my shoe flew off and went flying through the air. We punched, scratched, and pulled hair. I still don't know what I ever did to this girl to warrant her animosity, but she had an enormous dedication to upgrading her rank. I was attracting this kind of behavior without having even done anything. Summoning Zelda was the only way I knew how to handle physical threats.

At first, fighting was a last resort, a skill used to confront bullies and gain vindication for getting slapped in the face and strangled in public. But after each scuffle, the price was my self-respect. My conscience kept me up at night, replaying each savage act of violence on a loop and cycling images of me, a murderous, primitive cavewoman, blind with rage and unable to speak or use logic. I would have much rather been the type of person who could talk through problems and diffuse arguments with words. Yet my intense fear of physical harm outweighed my longing for tranquility, as some individuals seemed deserving of a swift and forceful reckoning upon their faces.

There's a reason the show *Yellowjackets* really resonates with me. High school was chock full of vipers, liars, and vampires, each with their own specific menagerie of puppets. I should have felt comfortable as a Leo in a lion's den, but I wasn't. My pseudo-friends and obsessive and unhealthy love interests taught me the importance of running bad relationships deep into the ground just to make sure I got everything I could out of them before they were buried. Otherwise, they'd just resurface after the wounds healed and a little time went by. Like the definition of insanity—doing the same thing over and over and expecting different results—I didn't want to get stuck on a never-ending merry-go-round of toxicity. Confronting the enemy was also much easier than battling my own internal demons, the ones who kept telling me I was unlovable, unintelligent, and ugly.

CHAPTER NINETEEN

THE FAMILY BREAKUP

My mom and I always found true connection by talking about her family. Unfortunately, the conversation stopped around 1988 when Mom started isolating herself on our balcony and sending me back inside to emotionally freeze to death. When pressed, she'd become tight-lipped and just say, "I don't want to talk about it. Go do your homework" or "why don't you go move the wash and fold the laundry."

I didn't understand the problem and was even more perplexed after I got an angry phone call from my cousin Shannon, acting as the family liaison who was investigating why they were all getting a cold shoulder from Mom. It had something to do with Christmas presents. I now know that creating space with her family was Mom's way of processing her past and essentially finding herself. But at the time, Shannon's mom, my Aunt Patsy, had manipulated my cousin into thinking I'd done something wrong, a common ploy to deflect guilt or blame.

I remember sitting on my mother's bed as she was getting ready for work one day. I asked, "Mom, did they send us something?" She grabbed some boxes wrapped in Christmas paper from the closet and put them down next to me. I opened the one with my name, which was written in scribbly letters by Bugger's shaky hand. Inside I found a thin, gold-plated bracelet. I called Shannon to thank her and said, "Oh, no! These are nice; I'm so sorry I'm just now seeing them." However, the phone call ended with Shannon calling me names and hanging up abruptly. That was the start of years of silence between Shannon and me. It was especially unfortunate because I could have used a big sister figure when I was in high school.

All those nights in silence on the balcony, Mom was listening to her special little voice, the one telling her that it was okay to be on her own and that she was going to be fine without them and without my dad. I was happy my mom was able to deal with her past, but I needed her in the present, especially at the height of my teen years when everything was confusing and new. During my crucial early elementary years, she had established the benchmark for being a supermom, which coincided with the peak of my cognitive, social, emotional, and physical growth. Adolescence was a lot more violent and moody than I ever expected, and Mom wasn't a supermom anymore; she was a human being with her own baggage.

I felt abandoned by both my parents. I felt like I didn't matter. All the while, Mom was suffering in her own head. Neither of us was communicating with the other; it was easier to just shut the door to our relationship than to address the pain we were both experiencing. I was insulted because I mistook her isolation for neglect.

I got my first paying job at People's Drugs (now CVS). I worked in the pharmacy, which encouraged my love of pharmaceutical drugs to flourish. Just a spoonful of medicine makes the pain go away! I learned to "straighten and face" store products, work the cashier desk up front, and assist in the pharmacy as needed. My boss was a middle-aged, White woman who was blind in one eye from being shot with an arrow by her brother. Her "good" eye was pale blue, and the iris of her "bad" eye was milky white. She made me watch her count down the cash registers every night. I couldn't leave until everything was clean and the cash matched the register's output. Any errors kept me from the best moment of my day, leaving work! I watched the clock like a hawk. Time always seemed to slow down the closer it got to the end of my shift, 10 p.m.

Working the register required quick math, which, as you already know, is not my strong suit, but I came up with little tricks to quickly figure out the change. Sometimes I'd round up the number in the customer's favor just to see if they'd notice, reduce the cost by a few dollars, or pretend to forget to ring up an item. The mood would strike when I'd see a friendly face, a tired mom, or a fellow teen employed at South Lakes shopping center. Eventually my boss caught me in the act, and I was swiftly fired. But working there taught me I couldn't escape math no matter what profession I pursued. It was also a great reminder of why going to college was so important and not to "Robin Hood" my employer.

CHAPTER TWENTY

THE BUMPER BUST

I wasn't getting my needs met at home, so high school is where I sought out inclusion and attention. Friendships became the lifeblood of my teenage years.

I met Samantha on my first day of class. She was a gorgeous, six-foot tall, platinum blonde with a sun-burnt orange perma-tan and glorious G-cup breasts. I envied those boobs. She came fully equipped with two close-knit friends, Dalia and Candice, and all three were similar in height and a year older than me. By the end of the semester, we'd all become so close that we made up our own sign language and gave each other old lady names. I was Gertrude, Samantha was Bertha, Dalia was Edith, and Candice was Mildred.

Dalia was Samantha's second-in-command, and I got a lot of resistance from her in the beginning. But after spending weeks skipping school to go on drive-bys to a house full of male college students at George Mason (the objects of their affection and obsession), I systematically endeared myself to these ladies. We listened to Mary J. Blige's "Real Love" so many times that we choreographed an upper body "chair dance" routine to it, acting out the words like we were interpreters. I felt like a mastermind for weaseling my way into their clique, and it was fantastic! Plus, having a bunch of older friends as tall as trees made me feel invincible.

Dalia was beautiful, with a round, half-Egyptian and half-French face. She changed her sibling's names from Chione and Horus to Chloe and Howard because those names sounded more American, and she wanted them to fit in. Her self-hatred was something I didn't understand because she was so pretty and skinny, like Kate Moss, who was blowing up at the time. Dalia worked at a trendy clothing store to help maintain her daily stylish ensembles, and she shielded me from where she lived until I was officially invited to join the inner circle. Like Bahija's house, I never saw the inside. The government-subsidized neighborhood that Dalia lived in was also home to a disfigured woman who suffered from goiters and always seemed to be lurking around during drop-off or pick-up. It was not the most pleasant neighborhood I had encountered.

One time, Dalia and I went on a beach trip to Ocean City, Maryland. Although we called it "Ocean Shitty" and didn't even bother to book a hotel room or pack bags, we hoped for the best. On the beach we met a nice group of attractive boys who were comparable in age, and we spent the evening playing cards and beer games and smoking cigarettes at the house the boys had rented for the week. It was getting late, and I worried about not having anywhere to sleep. I was on the brink of being too tired to drive back home. Luckily, the boys offered Dalia and me a bedroom with bunk beds. I took the bottom bunk and waited for Dalia. I waited and waited.

Dalia finally arrived in the wee hours of the morning, with a pile of clothes in her hand. She instructed me to open the window and climb out.

"Why?" I asked.

"So we don't wake them," she whispered.

I looked at her skeptically.

"Look, we need to leave now!" she said, then we jumped out of the window and drove away.

"Why did you steal their clothes?" I pressed, thinking they didn't deserve this after giving us beer and a place to sleep.

"Don't worry about it," she replied, leaving me to assume the worst. I thought she'd been roofied and/or raped; she couldn't have just been a laundry thief. We drove home, never speaking of it again.

Candice, the third-in-command, looked like an adorable, perfect Asian doll. She had been adopted by the Wallace family, and her sister, a quiet, shy, gorgeous blonde, was in my sisters class. And they became friends as well. The Wallaces lived in an enormous contemporary wooden house on the outskirts of Reston, with lots of modern appliances. Everything looked like it came out of the pages of a distinguished architectural magazine. This is what I loved about Reston: the four of us were an exciting mix of different cultures, physical features, nationalities, income levels, and religions, yet we were the best of friends. We laughed, loved, and got into trouble.

Candice and I set out to "shoulder tap" (to obtain beer by gently tapping a legal-age individual on the shoulder and presenting $20 upon entry) but found ourselves short on cash. We put our pea brains together and decided to steal two 45-ounce bottles, otherwise known in Reston as "bumpers," of Colt 45 Malt Liquor from the North Point Village Safeway instead. We stuffed the bottles underneath our winter jackets. Unfortunately, security saw us do it and two large male employees blocked our exit. However, the automatic sliding doors were much closer to me, and I made a break for them as the men closed in on me. I snuck past them like a slippery fish. Candice wasn't as graceful or fast. They picked her up and she tried to wriggle free but was overpowered and gave up. I couldn't leave her behind, so I surrendered too.

On the way back to the manager's office, we concocted another foolish plan. We pretended to be cousins from out of town visiting our mutual "Aunt Sofia," who was actually Samantha's older sister. We used fake names and phony accents for emphasis, mine from New Jersey and Candice's from Tennessee. We apologized profusely, hoping to acquire some goodwill, and it worked. They agreed not to press charges and let us go, leaving it in the hands of our relatives to punish or shame us sufficiently. The police drove us to our pretend Aunt Sofia's house, where I'd called Samantha in advance and, through code, arranged the drop-off and role play. I will be forever grateful that the masquerade worked and I was spared yet another month-long grounding.

These were the girls I chose to surround myself with. I loved them fiercely, just like I loved my cousins. They were fun, and I had no inhibitions with them. But none of us were a good influence on each other. It was always one kind of trouble or another.

CHAPTER TWENTY-ONE

BREATH CONTROL

In eighth grade, the South Lakes High School field hockey coaches came to Langston Hughes to recruit rising freshmen. We were given a stick and told to practice over the summer for the junior varsity tryouts in the fall. In August of 1989, I made the cut.

The team's coaches, Jamie Wellchase and Dawn Dorcus, put three stars on lofty pedestals: Collette Williams, Bridget Cameron, and Laura Sandusky. Like assorted Field Hockey Barbies varying in hair color—one blonde (Colette), one redhead (Laura), and one brunette (Bridget)—they helped newbies like me hone our skills by demonstrating technical maneuvers, such as how to dribble, flick, push, and force an obstruction, with perfect makeup and hot-rolled, bouncy hair. Everyone on the team worshipped them, including me. I loved swimming, but it was essentially a solitary sport, whereas field hockey transformed me into a vital part of a group. We were tough, unafraid young women.

I was always searching for a place where I belonged. I wanted a tangible identity, one associated with a term like "rockstar" or "jock."

My dreams of becoming a real "athlete," another option on the long list of cool descriptions I coveted, had finally come true! I loved the camaraderie and competition, and contact sports were the perfect outlet for my anger. Football players had helmets and protective pads, while we wore only a tiny rubber mouthguard and flimsy plastic shin guards, because we were fearless heroes . . . she-roes?

Laura in particular was my favorite Barbie. She was the most petite of the three Disney Princess champions. Her voice was even more adorable, with a tiny, barely audible lisp when she said words that ended in "s." My superlative would have been "team cheer-leader" or "most communicative." I was always shouting mantras and confidence boosters like, "Great Job! Nice hit! Way to go!" In class I pretended to have a slight lisp too, in the hope that boys would find me just as adorable as Laura. But when I went to an upperclassman party at my friend Buddy Harrison's house, where everyone, including Laura, completely ignored me, I dropped the lisp and my idolization vaporized.

After my second season, the coaches encouraged all the sopho-mores to go to field hockey camp over the summer, just to ensure we did everything we could to improve, because leveling up to varsity was imperative. Only three of us lasted until the end of camp due to its unsanitary practices. A virus spread through our barracks but spared me and two of my teammates. It was crazy how fast people got sick. It was almost like when Ebola came to Reston through a monkey strain, and 29 crab-eating macaques inexplicably died from a presumed airborne virus traveling through the ventilation system of Hazelton Labs.

The "monkey building" was located in Reston's Isaac Newton Square, the same location where I did my community service for the Woolworth's shoplifting incident, which was a month before the monkeys died, in the fall of 1989. Every day, I caught a RIBS bus (the Fairfax connector) filled with several other kids, mostly young

Black boys. One of them made me a colorful, beaded necklace I treasured so much that I wore it every day at camp, which gave me my first ever necklace tan line. None of us had any idea what was happening next door at the monkey building, but on the night of November 29, the army came dressed in hazmat suits to euthanize the remaining five hundred monkeys. Back then the information was mostly kept under wraps, until the book called *Hot Zone* by Richard Preston came out.

Back in our barracks, where the less life-threatening virus seemed to be jumping from bed to bed, we survivors were still forced to run from 6 a.m. to 6 p.m. in open fields under a merciless sun that caused blisters on our skin that would peel off in thick layers. This virus was not airborne; rather, the primary factor driving its rampant spread was the shortage of individual drinking cups. Each of the four fields had only one cup per water jug, and the antigen spread through saliva on the single cup hanging from the spout. Instead of using the cup, I always opted to use my hands. My friends and I felt extraordinarily strong when we didn't get infected. We also scored a ton of goals in our scrimmages and thought we had varsity in the bag.

When we came back for fall tryouts, our marathon-running coach made us play a cruel game called "Lap the Coach." We all lined up together at the starting line, but in order to "lap" Coach Wellchase, we needed to sprint a full lap ahead of her, which was impossible for me. I wasn't an endurance runner and barely lasted seven laps before needing to hyperventilate into a paper bag.

The next day I got cut from the team, and so did the other two camp survivors. According to Coach Wellchase, the coaches needed to make way for more promising sophomores and freshmen. I went into their office, bawling. "Could I just stay on JV?" I pleaded, since they had let one junior do this the year before. "I'm sorry, but no," they replied. I sobbed all night. My mom called the coaches and begged them to change their minds, reminding them of my learning disability to try to pull on their heartstrings and appeal to their human side. Mom's brilliant attempt to inspire a sympathetic response was rebuffed. They blew her off, unmoved.

Our school colors were blue and green, which complemented every complexion. I used to love school spirit days, until these coaches extinguished my spirit. But like Taylor Swift says, "Karma is a god." The next season, they lost almost every game. So much for talented fresh(man) meat.

Despite catching a reflection of my muscular back in the mirror, a result of the thousands of laps I swam in the pool, after I got cut from field hockey I decided to drop out of winter swimming as well so that I could focus on parties, drinking beer, and smoking cigarettes.

What I loved nearly as much as those activities (many times even more so) was music. Music was an escape from reality. I loved hearing my angst, anger, sadness, and story in the songs of others. "The Last Day of Our Acquaintance" by Sinéad O'Connor, a song about divorce, struck a giant nerve. I was drawn to the fury in Sinéad's voice; it was like melodic screaming with a Celtic twist. On my way to school, I'd listen to it over and over, sunroof down and volume as high as my '83 Oldsmobile Calais would allow, timing my approach into the parking lot with the entrance of the drums. I became obsessed with her melisma and use of trills. You can hear it when she says "anymore" in the phrase, "I know you don't love me anymore." She masterfully frolics with the break in her voice as well, as in the songs "The Foggy Dew" and "Never Get Old." These and many of her signature tricks are techniques I've been attempting to master (unsuccessfully) my entire life.

Singing is more than just a skill; it's a way of connecting with the world through music, and Sinéad O'Connor was the biggest troublemaker I could find. She was the real thing, a legitimate pro-test singer. Her incredible ability to translate genuine feelings into sound was so powerful it could restore hope to the suffering, give validation to anger, and be an outlet to release it. She was my first music therapist, and I worshipped her as an artist. I happened to be listening to her music when I wrapped my car around a telephone pole, the same thing that killed my Aunt Caroline 11 years prior.

CHAPTER TWENTY-TWO

BRONZED BEAUTY'S DEMISE

By my junior year, I'd already been suspended from school seven times for fighting. The majority of my troublemaking was due to my inability to use words to defuse violent altercations. The day my mom gave up and decided she didn't want me living with her anymore was the day of my eighth and last suspension for fighting.

Mr. Puffin was my favorite history teacher. He was six feet, five inches tall, looked like a Sumo wrestler, and wore suits that made him seem like a time traveler from the 1930s. His soft, feminine voice made it difficult to keep control over his classroom, even though everyone knew he could lift over eight hundred pounds. In a desperate attempt to get everyone's attention, he alluded to the (false) rumor that Catherine the Great died while having sex with a horse. My seat in his class was next to a picture of a terrified woman holding a baby and jumping off a cliff, a photo that perplexes me to this very day.

One afternoon, outside of Mr. Puffin's class, a large, portly upperclassman in a leg brace walked by on crutches. She stopped to give me a hateful look, lifted one crutch within one inch of my face, and said, "BEEYOTCH!" I'd never seen this girl before, but it didn't matter. Zelda took over.

Later, I was told that the big girl's name was Natasha. Apparently I had grabbed her crutch with both hands and put all my weight into it, knocking her off balance until she fell over backward. As she tumbled to the ground, I ripped the crutch out of her hands and beat her with it until Mr. Puffin came out from his classroom. He wrapped his giant arms around me from behind, in a snug bear hug. I screamed, "Stop! You're on my boobs!" thinking it would embarrass him enough to let me "finish the job."

This was part of a rage mentality that followed me throughout every violent encounter. Once my brain recognized a threat, I only saw red. With Zelda in control, the fight wasn't over until the opponent was either unconscious or dead. It was like I became a tiny version of myself, sitting in the machine operator booth, watching all the wheels, levers, and pedals move on their own. Mr. Puffin kept me restrained until Natasha was escorted away.

Mom left work early to pick me up from school but didn't want to hear anything about the argument or what happened because she didn't believe a word coming out of my mouth. We had just moved out of the rented townhouse in Hearthstone Court to a condo on the second floor of a building called Bristol House. It was the first home Mom had purchased on her own, which was quite an achievement, but nothing could have diffused her anger in that moment. I was grounded for a month, which included prom.

This fight was a metaphorical last straw. I thought I'd lost everything—my parents' love, their trust, my originality, my identity as an athlete, my way in life. I was tired of having no one in my corner. Everyone seemed to desert me when I needed them most.

At that fragile age, a nasty look from a stranger would destroy my self-worth, and every defeat was like the end of the world. Recognition for anything positive had been appropriated by my bad girl image. Mom didn't want me in the house. I didn't have anywhere else to go. Despite more than 20 attempts at begging my dad to let me move in with him, I wasn't welcome there either. He was too busy with his new family, his top priority. He'd say, "Just stick it out two more years, and then you'll be in college." Unfortunately, sticking it out was no longer an option for me.

I just wanted to go to sleep and leave everything else behind. With another night of instant-replay torture imminent, I decided to take matters into my own hands. I didn't want to die, but I also didn't really care if I did. I swallowed eight Unisom sleeping tablets and lay down in my new bedroom. After my sister found me uncharacteristically asleep at 5 p.m., she searched the bathroom trash and found the box of Unisom at the bottom. She did the math and called my dad, who rushed me to urgent care, where they gave me ipecac to induce brutal vomiting to force the poison out. I busted all the capillaries around my eyes, making me look like a dehydrated raccoon for days.

Dad and LeeAnn finally agreed to let me move in with them. I assumed the realization that I'd become a danger to myself prompted a change of heart. Dad went back to my mom's house the following day and found all my belongings in garbage bags outside the front door of Mom's new condo. I didn't even get a chance to pack up my own things. Mom had tossed them, and me, out.

Dad lived 20 minutes away from South Lakes High School and drove me back and forth for a week before realizing there was no way he could continue doing that. The silver lining, and the greatest gift of my teenage years, was the fact that living far from school meant I needed my own car—and I got one!

Samantha coined the car "Bronzed Beauty" due to its color—a shiny metallic bronze—and as an homage to our joint tanning addiction. Dad purchased the car from our neighbor. It came with tan leather seats, two doors, and a thin steering wheel made of sleek plastic, yet it was roomy enough to fit six passengers comfortably. I drove everywhere in that car; it was my ticket to freedom, including to and from school, and I'd even pick up Julie along the way. On the weekends I drove my friends to the beach and downtown Washington, DC.

I loved living in Dad's unfinished basement. It had a walkout with sliding glass doors, which made it convenient to sneak out of the house on school nights to hit up the cool dance clubs, such as Tracks, and our favorite underage watering hole, Quigley's. I had a cassette tape of "Rhythm is a Dancer" by Snap! that got stuck in the dash for over a month. I still love that song despite hearing it 5,478 times.

On Halloween, I drove to a hotel party in a neighboring town of Reston. I drank a couple beers and smoked a BUNCH of pot, blurring the details of nearly everything from earlier in the evening. I was going to my dad's house and got lost, which was pretty pathetic considering I was really only one town over.

Wet leaves covered every inch of the vacant road. I accidentally ran a stop sign and pressed the brakes in the middle of the vacant intersection and hydroplaned over a curb, onto the grass. In what felt like slow motion, I jumped from the driver's seat to the passenger seat, just before the car crashed into a telephone pole, which shattered the window and caved in the driver's side door. It was like I was having an out-of-body experience. Glass was everywhere and the door was jammed shut. I worried the car would explode, as I'd seen in movies, and jumped out the passenger side to hide behind a bush until I was convinced the car wouldn't spontaneously combust. Then I ran across the street to an industrial building and frantically ran around all four sides of it, looking for a pay phone, with no success. Conscious of the alcohol on my breath, I picked some foliage off a boxwood shrub lining the entrance and ate it. It was disgusting, but anything was better than cottonmouth. I was still very high.

It was 1 a.m. with no residential areas in sight. Luckily, a cop stopped by and phoned a roadside assistance truck instead of booking me for driving drunk. The tow truck arrived in minutes. I hopped onto the passenger seat and gave the driver my address. It didn't occur to me to have the car towed to a body shop.

Once at Dad's, I ran into the kitchen to chug milk to cure my cotton mouth and hopefully remove the pesticides still lingering on my tongue. I sobered up just in time for my dad to come downstairs. I told him I was in an accident but was okay. He seemed relieved until he found my demolished car in his driveway. He, understandably, was not happy about having to explain the situation to our neighbors.

In what seemed like an instant, I'd forfeited my integrity and my freedom by wrecking that car. I was lost, literally and metaphorically. I'd proven to everyone how untrustworthy I was; how irresponsible! I didn't dare tell my father I drove drunk and high, but I guess the cat's out of the bag now. Sorry Dad! I knew I could have killed myself, or worse, I could have killed someone else. I was so lucky to survive that crash. I was lucky I survived a lot of things during that period.

CHAPTER TWENTY-THREE

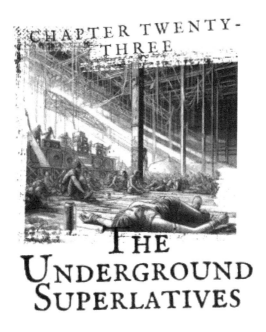

THE UNDERGROUND SUPERLATIVES

My brother Brandon was four when I moved in with Dad and LeeAnn. Every morning, he'd sneak down to the unfinished basement where I slept and say, "Wake up, Ellen! Take a shower!" and then giggle and run upstairs before I could catch him. I was living at Dad's house in Chantilly Highlands but was still able to go to the same high school, South Lakes. I needed something stable.

I was still in my junior year when Samantha and I met up with some of our guy friends—Bryce, Allen, and Danny—to go to my first (and last) rave in Maryland. On the way to catch a bus out of Baltimore, we stopped at McDonald's, where I bought a fountain soda and replaced the contents with beer.

The bus drove for miles without any streetlamps. We came upon a warehouse in a remote area, surrounded by a huge parking lot. As we approached the building, 30-foot electronic doors began to open, and multicolor laser lights flooded the parking lot and darted into the bus. Inside the warehouse, people were dancing all around in little patches. The dancers near the entrance scattered through strobe lights and fog to get out of the way. To our surprise, the bus drove all the way inside, and the gargantuan doors lowered to the ground behind us.

We exited the bus and made our way to the makeshift bar. I didn't trust my fake ID, which I'd borrowed from a friend, a Puerto Rican blonde named Gabriela, so I waited on the dance floor for my older friends to buy me another beer. The bass was so loud that the ground and all the bones in my body trembled. A skater boy with greasy brown hair and baggy clothes approached and asked if I wanted a "hit" from the tiny shot glass filled with clear liquid he was holding. I assumed he'd said, "Drink this," so I took the little cup from his hands. He warned me, "Don't let it touch your lips," which should've forced me to take pause. But it didn't. Instead, I reasoned it just tasted as bad as it smelled—a strong mix of 409, sweaty socks, and penicillin—and slung the entire cup's contents into the back of my throat.

My friends appeared just as the boy's expression changed from excitement to pure dread. He shouted, "That was Rush; it's an inhalant!"

Now it was my turn to panic. The next bus arrived, and the enormous doors reopened. I ran outside like a cat seeking a place to die and spotted an area covered in urine on the asphalt (although it might have been gasoline). Having just learned about the ancient Romans who valued urine for its ammonia content and used it to sterilize and clean, I decided it was the perfect place to faint.

I'm not sure how much time passed after I collapsed. When I came to, my friends were ushering me onto the next bus headed to Baltimore. I still had the McDonald's cup! By the time we reached our car, I'd filled it to the rim with poisoned spit. Once again, I knew how lucky I was to have survived my own stupidity.

Back at high school, the jocks were responsible for writing and publishing the "Underground Superlatives," a ghastly list you did not, under any circumstances, want to be on. Yearbook superlatives were supposed to be cute, hyperbolic expressions of praise. I'm hoping they've changed in recent years, because during my senior year, the only other Ellen in my class got the title of "Best Legs," which meant, by default, I was "Ellen with the Bad Legs."

When I was a freshman in high school, I saw a senior get so drunk at McDonald's—a place where hundreds of kids swarmed, blasting music through DIY customized sound systems—that she did a lap dance in front of the entire football team, completely ignoring the puddle of yellow urine running down her white pants. Another girl took a muscle relaxer right before she passed out behind a couch at a party and shat herself in her sleep, but these two were spared.

The disparaging Underground Superlatives list was reserved for girls who did anything to piss off the jocks, including refusing sex or rejecting them in any way. Their retribution was malicious slander. Embarrassing a boy was an incredibly dangerous offense. The list of mudslinging titles included "Best at Sucking Dick," "Class Whore," "Butterface," and "Most Likely to Have a Lifelong STD." No holds barred, they could write anything to ruin your reputation for the unforeseeable future. I received two titles:

1. "Most Likely to Not Graduate"
2. "Class Alcoholic"

The first was nearly a self-fulfilling prophecy. The second stemmed from learning how to drink around these assholes. Sure, sometimes I'd forget my limits, but who didn't? I might have chugged vodka and rolled down a hill at the "Broken Rim," an industrial park we'd frequent when we couldn't find a house party (and was named for a broken basketball hoop in the parking lot), but I was fun, and everyone followed me. Maybe they were just jealous of my drunken leadership qualities. If anything, I brought the party up to the next level on the fun spectrum. I never cried, threw up on anyone, or got violent, at least not when I was drinking. I took great pride in being the "happy drunk" of my friend's circle. Though in the early '90s, being the life of the party or too much of anything—too fun, too outspoken, too brave—were skills reserved for boys. I guess I just didn't like staying in my place.

CHAPTER TWENTY-FOUR

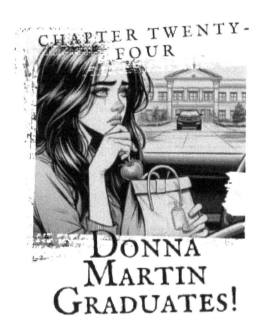

DONNA MARTIN GRADUATES!

South Lakes High School was broken down into subschools and corresponding cafeterias: green for freshmen, blue for sophomores, yellow for juniors, and orange for seniors, all ripe for fighting. As a senior, I'd stroll over to the green cafeteria to tease my sister Julie, but in reality my visits were calculated to tip off her classmates that anyone who dared to give her shit would be annihilated. She'd feign embarrassment but secretly loved the recognition. Her teachers, on the other hand, registered our same last name and sent her to the principal's office before she could prove to any of them that she was the good one.

LeeAnn bought me the most beautiful clothes for Christmas that year: a short red pleated skirt made of silky rayon, a black and red plaid sweater, nude pantyhose, and red flats. I couldn't wait to show them off to my new, valedictorian boyfriend, Matthew Valentino, whose aristocratic parents helped him get ahead in life. His father was a Yale grad who read Greco-Roman mythology to Matthew instead of nursery rhymes, and his mother taught him to speak and write in fluent German, her native tongue. He received a perfect score on his SATs and was the star of the lacrosse team and the German club.

On picture day, I practiced my smile in the mirror and tried to memorize the exact feeling in my muscles to make the most flattering face. I filled out my yearbook form, acknowledging the field hockey and swim teams in ninth and tenth grade as well as concert, jazz, acapella, and madrigal choirs. I left two quotes: "It's time I was on my way / Thanks to you I'm much obliged / For such a pleasant stay" by Led Zeppelin and from the movie Hellraiser III, "Go ahead! What, ya think you're gonna live forever?"

During LD class, my teacher gave me a pink hall pass allowing me to walk around school requesting college recommendations from my other teachers. However, this was during semifinals, and teachers were stationed at each subschool to ensure kids didn't try to skip out. I noticed one teacher giving me the side-eye as I passed into the yellow subschool on my way to Mr. Bernhard's biology class. Mr. Bernhard was my best bet for a glowing endorsement. I flashed my pass to the angry redhead stationed behind her desk and walked into the classroom.

I got a bad feeling when I saw all the students inside with their heads down in concentration. Mr. Bernhard was nowhere to be found, but a teacher's assistant got up from behind the desk with a tut-tut attitude to shoo me away. I turned, exited the classroom, and ran into the redheaded woman who was standing in the hallway, waiting for me. I figured that since I'd made my approved intentions clear, my pink pass should've ended our encounter. Boy was I wrong!

I walked toward the stairs, ignoring the invisible daggers ejecting from the creepy teacher's eyes. She said nothing but followed closely behind. As I entered the stairwell through the double doors, she caught one before it swung shut behind me. Then she charged full speed ahead of me up the stairs. When she got near the top of the landing, she turned to confront me.

"Excuse me!" she hissed in a hostile German accent. "Vat are you doing?"

She was so close to my face that I could see the pores on her skin, which looked like worm-holed wood. I shouted back, "You saw this pass, right?" and held it up to her loathsome face. "I'm going back to my class!" I insisted. She didn't like that.

I continued up the stairs closest to the railing. She backpedaled up another step, put her hands on my chest, and shoved me. This was when I realized I was in danger and she was actually trying to push me down the stairs. I instinctively grabbed the railing and pushed back hard. I climbed another step toward her for leverage, forcing her to trip backward over the top stair, where she landed on her ass. Everything happened in a nanosecond, but I knew instantly that I was in a world of trouble. Everything was upstairs, including my classroom, my principal, and my subschool. I needed to get up one more flight of stairs to clear my name to the only person left in my corner, my advisor, Mr. Traidon.

I tried to run around the woman, but she was like a spider monkey. She scrambled to get up by grabbing my ankle! "Vere are you going?" she hissed from the floor.

I didn't understand or have time to process why this woman was going after me. "I already told you, I'm going back to class! Get off of me!" I shouted, then fought the urge to kick her while she was down. I extricated my leg free by shaking and twisting it, forcing her to loosen her simian grip. Upon liberation, I sprinted up the next flight of stairs, opened the door, and bolted down the hallway toward my subschool principal's office, where Mr. Traidon was sitting at his desk.

I shut the door behind me and breathlessly told my story through a constant stream of tears and hyperventilation. He told me to calm down, handed me a pen and paper to record what happened, and told me he'd be right back. I assumed he went to check the stairwell and find the woman I'd just described, whose name turned out to be Frau Unhöflich. And Matthew just happened to be her star student.

None of the details in my verbal and written story ever changed. Frau Unhöflich's story wasn't nearly as consistent, but it didn't matter because she was given a platform to share her fabricated narrative first, to everyone on staff at South Lakes during an emergency staff meeting organized by Mr. Traidon. Frau Unhöflich, likely embarrassed by her erratic, crazy behavior, falsely accused me of pushing her down a flight of stairs and kicking her in the chest. One or two of my teachers spoke up in my defense, but they were overruled by the erroneous, frightening testimony that aligned perfectly to another situation that had the community up in arms. Four teenagers had terrorized the teachers at our rival high school, Herndon, just a few weeks earlier. The news was abuzz, and Frau Unhöflich seized the opportunity to escalate fear by working in collaboration with the principal, another German individual named Dr. Schmucker.

After the incident, I waited for Matthew to call, but he never did. I sat home for months waiting for the school to figure out what to do with me and started to make the connection between Matthew's mother, the German club, the German teacher, and the German principal. Had Matthew's mother pretended to like me insincerely? Was it she who tipped Frau Unhöflich and Dr. Schmucker off about my lack of pure Aryan blood? I started to suspect I was being singled out for being Jewish because it was the only way to make sense of the attack, but no one believed me. My history of violent behavior provided too much evidence to warrant giving me the benefit of the doubt.

Dr. Schmucker and Frau Unhöflich wanted to have me expelled, but in Fairfax County they can't kick you out permanently unless you're found guilty of assault and convicted in a court of law. Had I actually been guilty, I would have been forced to go to a private or military school. My case was dismissed in my favor when Frau Unhöflich failed to provide reliable and consistent testimony and medical records for her fake injuries, despite having Dr. Schmucker by her side in the courtroom.

Sadly, going back to South Lakes was no longer an option, as Dr. Schmucker would have been ousted for circumventing due process by letting an anti-Semitic fraud usurp the school board's soap box. Needless to say, I didn't get any college recommendations and was given a choice of three schools closest to our home to finish out my senior year: Herndon High School, Oakton High School, or Chantilly High School. As I mentioned earlier, Herndon's reputation for violence was worse than that of South Lakes. The colleagues at my recently acquired job at Crest Cleaners in Franklin Farm, where my father lived, were all Oakton students. They warned me that I wouldn't blend in with the affluent, elitist crowd. So Chantilly was the only remaining viable option.

South Lakes failed me. It literally failed me by flunking me out of every class, and it metaphorically failed me by letting the injustices (from whom I predicted at the time to be a deranged Nazi) influence my fate. I had no idea who this Frau Unhöflich woman even was, but it was clear she wanted to take me down. In hindsight, it seems like it was a deliberate plot to get me. Regardless, I knew it was time to make some major changes if I wanted to graduate and fulfill my dreams of becoming someone important in the world.

Decades later, I was at a birthday lunch for a friend and seated next to another South Lakes alumni, Mary, whose oldest sister is a New Jersey congresswoman. I was retelling the story of getting kicked out of South Lakes and referenced the *Beverly Hills: 90210* episode "Donna Martin Graduates" (officially titled "Something in the Air"). Everyone laughed except for Mary, who didn't know the backstory. When I brought her up to speed about the altercation with Frau Unhöflich, she said, "OMG, she was my teacher!" She vividly recalled a paper she'd written discussing the atrocities of Nazi Germany. Frau Unhöflich had handed her back the paper, which was covered in red pen, and commented, "You shouldn't talk about things you don't understand." Ah-ha! Vindication! It was obvious to everyone at the table that I'd been correct in my assumptions.

In the four weeks I spent at home waiting to go back to school, I fell miles behind in my classes. At Chantilly, my government teacher showed mercy by allowing me to use my previous government class paper about Reston as a substitute for the class project. Even back then, the more I learned about Reston, the more I was able to confirm how special it was. I also thought it would be fun to educate my new classmates about their neighboring town, although at the time I couldn't wait to get out of both Chantilly and Reston. I believed I was destined for bigger things and a better life somewhere else.

My first week at Chantilly was rough. I didn't make a single friend and ate lunch in my car so I could cry in private. I wore a lot of gray to be anonymous and was determined not to become a dropout loser. I had to make it to graduation without making waves and get over the grievance of being exiled from everything and everyone I knew. I was SO JEALOUS of Donna Martin. Not the Donna Martin who'd moved into my old house on Tanbark Drive, although I was deeply bitter when she took my place, but the Donna Martin from *Beverly Hills: 90210* who was in jeopardy of not graduating from West Beverly High because she was caught drinking on prom night. The whole school arranged a protest in her honor, chanting, "Donna Martin graduates! Donna Martin graduates!" Alas, I didn't have anyone chanting in my corner.

Though I'd gone to three schools on the same block with the same people for almost 13 years, no one batted an eyelash at my departure, which made it feel like everyone was glad to see me go. To add insult to insult, Donna Martin from Tanbark was graduating from South Lakes—from *my* high school, with *my* friends. Everything seemed backward and upside down.

CHAPTER TWENTY-FIVE

CAFETERIA KARMA

After two weeks of eating lunch in my car, my guidance counselor at Chantilly realized I wasn't eating in the cafeteria and didn't have any friends. I was assigned a lunch buddy, a cute junior named Marvin from my choir class. One day, soon after the prescribed lunch arrangement, a girl named Hillary Knox walked up to me in the cafeteria. She asked my name and where I was from, then invited me to her table, telling me about all her cool friends that I was about to meet. This, to me, was karma in full force. Back in eighth grade, I had extended the same courtesy to Danielle. I hoped that this was the universe's way of telling me I had done something good once, and it was now coming back to me.

After forging a relationship with Hillary, I became a person of interest. People wanted to know why I was there with only four months left till graduation. It was the first thing everyone asked me. The easy copout responses were, "My parents moved" or "I just started living with my dad." Eventually, my network of friends extended to the cool boys, and their leader, Tony, invited me to his party. I remember chatting on the stairs of his deck, where all the mean cheerleader girls swarmed around to interrogate me, skillfully sugarcoating their questions with artificial innocence. "But why now, so close to graduation?" they asked, acting dumb. *Dumb like foxes*, I thought. I felt obligated to be forthright, but I also wanted them to sense the undercurrent of threat and understand that if pushed hard enough, I could beat the shit out of them. Luckily, it worked and they left me alone.

I just had to make it through four months at Chantilly to graduate. I made some friends, was doing my schoolwork, and wasn't a total delinquent. I was still a fighter, but now I was fighting for my rights. I didn't want to be a fuck-up, and I was determined to show everyone that I could fight my way to the top, which is exactly what I did. I may not have graduated with the friends I grew up with and had known my entire life, I may not have graduated from the high school I started at, but I got straight As my last quarter and I graduated. I walked, I wore a cap and gown, and I got my high school diploma. Things were looking good.

PART

III

Once you grow up, you can never go back.

- BOSS BABY 2

CHAPTER TWENTY-SIX

GREEK ORIENTATION

I based my decision on what colleges to apply to on four factors:

1. The university must have the name of a state in it, for brand recognition, and a good Division I football team, for bragging rights.

2. It must be a Southern school so I could be the first in my family to experience the Deep South and fight (and conquer) anti-Semitism and racism.

3. It must be a school that would accept me. Pickings were slim given my mediocre grades, early dismissal from South Lakes High School, and pathetically low SAT scores.

4. It must be far enough away to make me feel like I was on my own but close enough to drive home in one day's time, just in case the South turned on me as it had in Reston. Like Ruth B., who sang, "As we soared above the town that never loved me," I wanted to fly away from my hometown and anyone in it. I was going to start over. Again.

I got accepted to three schools: Radford, Alabama, and the University of Tennessee (UT). I was rejected by the ones that didn't wait for my last quarter of grades: West Virginia University and East Carolina University. Had I not been kicked out of South Lakes, I would have gone to Radford with the same toxic people I was close to at the time and the first ones to desert me after I was removed. Alabama was my first choice initially, but once I realized it was double the cost (16k a year) and twice the commute (16 hours away), I chose UT, which was only 8k a year and 8 hours away, instead.

The idea of being the new girl from a faraway land gave me confidence. It would be a new beginning, with new people and new experiences. I never would have dreamed of going so far away before getting kicked out of high school. But surviving all the trauma associated with that and being forced to finish my senior year elsewhere proved to me that I could do it; I could make friends, I could get along with teachers, and I could be successful. Now it was time to do all those things in college.

I hadn't even seen a picture of the campus before I applied, and I knew nothing about the school or the state, except that the school met my criteria. But I was accepted and showed up for my orientation in August 1993. My mom and I were making strides to reconnect, and she accompanied me on the drive in my "new to me" '85 Oldsmobile Calais, which was white with a gray interior. It even had a cell phone installed by the previous owner in the console who never disconnected the service, which came in super handy on our way home when the timing chain broke. The car was essentially totalled, but the relationship between mom and me was finally improving. I had graduated from Chantilly and was on my way to college. This was something she had always wanted for me.

At orientation, we attended an hour-long presentation about sororities. All I knew about Greek life prior to that was from my dad, who'd been the president of his fraternity, Sigma Alpha Mu (otherwise known as Sammy), a Jewish fraternity at Penn State. He loved being part of a group known as "the nice guys." In 1970, there were a total of 63 fraternities, and only six of those were Jewish. My dad is now 75 years old and is still in contact with many of his frat brothers. Most of his fond memories involve the friends he met in Sammy, like "Sammy Jammies," when they had bands come to the frat house for parties, or the time they failed a health inspection that found 37 violations in the attic alone. The house was condemned shortly after, but not before my dad's frat brother drove a motorcycle through the house.

I imagined what wild stories I'd be able to tell my kids someday but then lost interest in the presentation after hearing about the $1,000 per year fee and the use of an exhaustive set of evaluations. To me, this meant the payment should go the other way around. I harshly judged anyone willing to subject themselves to this insane level of scrutiny. Even if I could have afforded the cost, which I couldn't, it would not have guaranteed admission to the sorority of my choice. Plus, they didn't have any Jewish sororities at UT. They still don't.

I've always been outgoing and confident in my ability to secure meaningful relationships, especially after the transfer from South Lakes to Chantilly, and I knew I'd be okay on my own. I also remembered a story my dad shared about a fraternity president's meeting where he'd struck up a conversation with the president of Sigma Nu (the frat for jocks), Patrick McKenna. When Patrick heard Dad was a Sammy, he looked at him in disbelief and asked, "You're Jewish?" Then he peeked around Dad's backside and then inspected his forehead. Dad replied, "Yes, and what the hell are you doing?" Patrick said he was checking for horns and a tail because he was told growing up that Jews had horns and tails. My dad thought it was hilarious, and they ended up becoming close friends.

I always kept that story in the back of my mind for when I contemplated revealing my Jewish identity to a new person. Greek life wouldn't be for me.

CHAPTER TWENTY-SEVEN

EGG NOODLES

One of my best college friends, Lainey, recalled the moment her father dropped her off at UT when she eulogized him at his funeral decades later. She recalled the intensity of her nerves and how her dad tried to soothe them by saying, "You know, you don't have to do this. I can turn this car around right now, and we can go back home and come up with a new plan together." Lainey wanted to be brave but was grateful to have a father who knew her so well. The tender gesture made her tear up, but they kept going. Her father probably knew Lainey wouldn't succumb to the appeal of turning around, to go back to the safety nest of home, but he recognized the fact that neither of them was 100 percent ready to let go of each other. Her dad's vulnerability gave Lainey the opportunity to be strong, to help her realize it was her time to grow up and be on her own, and to advance their parent–child relationship into its next chapter.

My college drop-off was a little different. I definitely was not given an option to back out. There was nowhere else to go. Dad drove, and Julie tagged along for the eight-hour trek. They helped me carry my suitcases into the dorm room, where I met my first roommate ever, Marnie Abbott from Chattanooga. Afterward, Dad and Julie sped out the door as fast as they had come in, saying goodbye with dry eyes. They hugged me, turned around, and walked out the door. I watched them walk the length of the long hallway and turn left around the corner to the elevators. It was at that moment I felt my throat closing. I squeezed out a soft, squeaky whimper while my heart sank. Never once did they look back. Never once.

My new, redheaded suitemate, Gloria, found me crying softly to myself in the doorway. She asked, "Hey, are you okay?"

"I'm just emotional because I know my life will never be the same," I replied.

I lived on the eighth floor of the South Carrick girls' dormitory and scored the worst GPA average since my transfer out of South Lakes, a pathetic .08. It didn't help that I skipped morning classes to sleep in. Waiting until the last minute to register for classes had been a colossal mistake. Back then, the options to register were either through the arduous task of physically showing up to wait in line at that registrar's office or via phone into a slow, archaic system using a thick reference book and requiring hours of prework to gather class numbers. I landed French II at the excruciatingly early hour of 8 a.m. If I hadn't stayed up all night drinking coffee and playing cards, 8 a.m. would've been fine. My priorities were skewed.

I didn't know anyone else in the entire state of Tennessee, so my first goal was to connect with and make new friends quickly. I had initially set out to prove everyone wrong by prioritizing my school-work and attendance. Those priorities quickly got downgraded to the bottom of the list. The result was new friendships galore but learning virtually nothing my freshman year, forcing me to take each class over during a "super senior" year, a.k.a. an expensive fifth year of college.

Most girls had the same desire: to shed our childlike naivety and become the mature, sophisticated, independent adults we were destined to be. We began our journey at night, meeting for gab sessions over a casual card game called Spades, where we downed multiple pots of coffee. Like crackheads playing cards for more crack, I drank so much coffee that I eventually burned a hole in my insides, an ulcer so painful that I didn't drink coffee again until I had kids (and subsequently walked around my house sleepily, like a ghost of my former self). We seized every opportunity to bond and to party, 24/7. Over time, we learned to signal each other, count cards, and become good enough to enter a tournament, where we beat out all the other teams from the eighth floor. We got first place in our dorm, beating out the 12 other floors in South Carrick, and ultimately we placed third against all the other dorms at UT.

The chaotic transition from home to college during my freshman year generated the most crazy-ass, graphic dreams. I started a dream journal and kept it bedside to scribble images and descriptions to make sense of what my subconscious was picking up during the day. I wanted to be wholly conscious, I guess. Vivid dreams can be a result of fragmented sleep, which is a symptom of my struggle with insomnia, but it can also be caused by stress, drugs, alcohol, pregnancy, or certain medical conditions. My brain was very active during sleep that year, which unfortunately left me brainless during waking hours and caused me to almost flunk out of school.

During these restless nights, I dreamed about things like swallowing shrimp that came back to life halfway down my throat, getting a rat bite, running from serial killers, seeing burned flesh on a stick, and being chased by a 60-foot snake while swimming in Lake Audubon. I'd dream about my cousin Shannon and the inflatable purple-and-blue bunnies we got for Easter, and I'd dream about Dave Matthews, my mother, Hitler, mean cheerleaders, *90210*, and homes from childhood with inverted floor plans. I'd also dream about falling through a ceiling, being fat-shamed by my family, confronting two former high school friends (Ronnie and Brett) who'd committed suicide, and attending pro-choice rallies like the one my mom and Sue Krause took me to in middle school with my friend Josephine. And then there was lightning, lots of violence, vomit, and wild sex.

They say real events or images seep into your subconscious and come back to you in your dreams to remind or signal you. Dreams are more frequent and vivid when you're in a stage of adjustment. Moving eight hours away from home to a state with a completely different landscape, dialect, and culture was the biggest adjustment I'd ever made.

My new friends Sloane and Jocelyn were so pretty that their high school classmates festooned them with homecoming and prom queen crowns four years in a row. We first met on the shared floor of our dorm in the room of a girl named Sadie, who looked like a life-sized Tinkerbell, complete with red hair in a European-styled pixie cut, freckles, green eyes, and a small, ballerina-like frame. My suitemates, Gloria and Marnie, were acquainted with Sadie and were part of the Chattanooga group that occupied half of the dorm.

On the night we met, Sadie asked me to hold off on lighting a joint until Jocelyn and Sloane, who were from Lafayette, Tennessee, arrived. When they walked in the door, I thought they were dizzyingly beautiful and braced myself for mean girl jokes. Both were moderately short and had gymnast builds from cheerleading in high school. We sat in a circle and talked about where we were from.

The joint had gone around a couple times when I heard a faint knock on the door. "Did you hear that?" I asked.

Sloane answered, "No, but you have big ears."

I looked at her deadpan face.

Jocelyn interjected, "She's just fucking with you; your ears are normal."

We went back to our conversation. Sloane told me "Ellen" was too hard for Southern people to say and decided to change my name to Helen. A few minutes later she said, "You do have good hearing; must be your giant ears."

I lost my patience. "What is your deal, lady?" I asked in a less than pleasant tone. Apparently, this was how Sloane made new friends.

Sloane had six majors over the course of the next six years, including drama, chemistry, math, film studies, political science, and computer science. She used to get drunk and slap everyone in the face, but she was so cute that no one got angry or retaliated. She'd roll down the window and yell, "Hey, who ordered the prostitutes?" to anyone—guys, girls, groups, actual hookers, it didn't matter. She also called grown men "boys," and everyone was "brown-headed" instead of brunette, "blonde-headed" instead of blonde, and "the devil" instead of redheaded. To her, all redheads were angry, aggressive, and ugly and (she always added this at the end for good measure) "should not be allowed to live." She believed this up until the time she gave birth to a beautiful redheaded baby girl. Karma.

Jocelyn had a four-foot-tall poster of Shannon Hoon from Blind Melon on her wall and cried for three days after his death from an overdose in 1995. Sloane, on the other hand, was obsessed with John (Cougar) Mellencamp. She had sex dreams about him and wanted to have his babies. On the wall of her dorm room, she hung "The Truth of Your Horoscopes," which had wild descriptions of each sign. One was, "Leo—the adventurous type, always looking for thrills and willing to try anything. In other words, stupid. You have the IQ of a garden snail and will never amount to anything. Most Leos are on welfare." Another was, "Gemini—your sign denotes an air of duality in your character. Simply, you are a neurotic schizophrenic. A real weirdo, the type of person who'd kill themselves to win a bet." My favorite was, "Sagittarius—you are the romantic mushy type, soft-hearted, and a lover of the arts. You are likely to import Dutch pornography and sex toys. You will die a virgin."

Jocelyn had olive skin, light brown hair, and bright-green eyes. She said her mother's dad was part Melungeon, a mysterious race from the Appalachians who were rumored to be French Polynesian soldiers and coupled with Native Americans, likely Cherokee—the tribe my mom's dad claimed to be a part of and who ran for the hills to avoid the Trail of Tears, settling in North Carolina and Tennessee. Sloane had big, blonde, country hair, and bright, enormous, blue eyes, accentuated by copious amounts of mascara that looked like a million spiders hatching from her eyelids. She was a very skilled gymnast who dabbled in contortion and biomechanics to perform backbends while I stood on her pelvic bones, an amazing party trick.

Jocelyn was the oldest of four girls, and every member of her family had names that started with "J." There were her sisters Jamie, Joanna, and Jane, and their parents were Jeanine and Joshua. When I visited their home, they performed what it was like in church when someone spoke in tongues and took me spelunking in the caves behind their backyard. Their house was full of laughter, and they were silly with each other. This was completely different from my home life.

I loved everything about Sloane and Jocelyn. Our friendship was so different for me, so different from all the dysfunction I had experienced in my teenage friendships.

The first summer in college, I stayed in Knoxville for a few weeks with my boyfriend at the time, Greg Swantree from Hendersonville. Greg was an engineering major whom I met in choir. He was tall, funny, and very handsome, with the most adorable dimples and shiny black hair. His parents lived in an affluent neighborhood, right next door to Reba McEntire and Johnny Cash, so I'm not sure why Greg was living in such squalor at UT. His house was a shack, and he shared the second-floor apartment with a roommate who dealt mushrooms and weed to pay for college.

Knoxville was a ghost town in the summer. The only students who stuck around were the bar and restaurant workers. Greg and I took a few shifts at Olive Garden together, but all our coworkers loved him and made their disdain for me increasingly impossible to ignore. When I pointed it out to Greg, we got into a huge fight. I went to my efficiency at Shelbourne Towers, or as we referred to it, "Hellbourne" Towers, alone for the first time since I'd put down the security deposit. I attempted to lift my spirits by inventing a pretext to have friends over, to distract me from my loneliness. "I'm having a dinner party," I said when I called Jocelyn and Sloane.

My apartment had a collection of donated items, including a twin bed that was actually the bottom half of my old bunk bed from Tanbark Drive and an ancient folding card table (which I still have) that sat the three of us comfortably. I served boiled egg noodles with butter and salt, and to drink, a six-pack of Milwaukee's Best. No appetizer, hors d'oeuvres, sides, or dessert. "I'm sorry," I said. "This is the only thing I know how to make."

"I love noodles!" Jocelyn replied.

"Cooking lessons start this week," Sloane said. "This is sweet, but just pitiful, Helen."

Greg and I made up the next day when he came to Hellbourne with gifts in hand, a beautiful butter-yellow floral print sundress and a kelly-green sweater. I took him back. I wasn't ready to live on my own just yet.

With the fragile state of my security now more apparent than ever, I went home to work on my relationship with Mom. On this particular visit, and moving forward, I was extended an invitation to join her out on the balcony. I introduced her to a new bands like Stone Temple Pilots, Alice in Chains and Pearl Jam; however, she did not care for them. I spilled my guts and let out a relentless stream of complaints about how hard my classes were and how difficult it was to be organized and navigate the campus, culture, and professors. I wanted to give up. Like Edie Brickell sings in "Circle," "I quit / I give up / Nothing's good enough for anybody else, it seems."

I wanted my mom to tell me it was okay to come home, but she didn't. Instead, she said, "Ellen, you're a brave and intelligent young woman. You know deep down that you'll regret it for the rest of your life if you don't finish school and graduate. I believe in you. You can do this!"

Like magic, the impactful pep talk put everything back in perspective. I was determined not to let anything get in my way again. I even found shortcuts, like retaking English and biology at Northern Virginia Community College over the summer. These were the two classes at UT designed to weed out Freshman students by setting the minimum roster at one hundred, a challenge at which I'd failed miserably. I needed more attention and it was hard to focus with so many people in one room.

There was just one stipulation to living at Mom's condo: I needed to go to anger management therapy. Also, she offered me a two-week internship at her company, HunterLab. I had to sort through files and organize them alphabetically. This was around the time we heard about the pending destruction of the monkey building less than a mile down the road and asked her photographer to accompany us for a photo shoot to document the historic event. We stood out in front of the monkey building and put our hands around our necks as if we were choking, convinced we were hilarious.

The mental gymnastics involved in therapy were to identify my source of irritation, my degree of anger, and the other person's role and to count to 10 before speaking or leaving the room. The signs for recognizing anger were an increased heart rate, tense muscles, and racing thoughts. The techniques to control anger were to reframe the event, think of how the other person would want me to respond, take deep breaths, write in a journal, take a walk, stretch, and think about something joyful or calmly repeat the phrase "relax." All of these techniques came in handy at some point, but I still viewed the sessions as punitive, just like when I was nine and felt unmoored from other things I could be doing that I actually enjoyed.

CHAPTER TWENTY-EIGHT

BAD PHOTOSHOP

The following school year, I hung out with the same crew from my freshman days: Greg, Jocelyn, and Sloane. Jocelyn's thick accent only accentuated her formidable beauty. Due to constant praise, onlookers everywhere we went, and the supermodel phenomenon of the '90s era, she developed modeling aspirations and met a sleazy photographer named Mike who conned us both into a photoshoot. I was only playing wingwoman to her dreams, but I was happy to be dragged along as protection.

We showed up on-site to an upscale restaurant called The Orangery on Kingston Pike, arriving with multiple dresses as instructed. Mike combed through them to find the most revealing. After we donned the scanty dresses, he ushered us outside with suitcases and photographed us holding them, posed like hitchhikers on the highway. For the next photoshoot, he promised to bring our headshots to help us start a portfolio.

The next site for said photoshoot was located on a picturesque ranch with gardens overlooking scenic mountain views. At first sight, we thought it might be a legitimate operation because there were racks of costumes and props spread all over the lanai. The photographers were all middle-aged White men, and young, beautiful girls were scattered around the premises. One photographer was assigned to each young girl, including us. I feared for my friend but acquiesced after she insisted she'd be fine.

My assigned photographer instructed me to pick up some flowers, then led me to a hammock (sigh) and told me to sit down and tilt my head back: "Like you're bathing in sunshine," he said. Then he asked me to remove my shirt.

"No thank you, but fuck you very much," I muttered, channeling Ani DiFranco, before bolting back to the lanai where I'd last seen Jocelyn.

Jocelyn was standing there alone, with a look on her face that matched my feelings of disgust. Turns out we were the only girls who refused to pose naked. She asked me where Mike went. I said, "I don't know, but he probably went into the woods to rub one off. Let's get the hell out of here."

A couple of weeks later we went to pick up our headshots at Mike's apartment. His weird, redheaded girlfriend had just come out of the shower and was walking around his apartment in a towel, making us want to puke at whatever Mike did to make her feel dirty. We sat uncomfortably at his kitchen table. Naked pictures of this woman lined the walls of Mike's apartment. I whispered, "Blink twice if you need help." Jocelyn laughed.

Mike sat down and produced a single 8 x 10 photo of Jocelyn with a black scarf covering her head, like he was going for a *National Geographic* look. He fed us a bunch of bullshit about how difficult it is to get started in this business. We got up and left abruptly. On the ride home, Jocelyn tore up the picture and threw it out the window, pieces of her lovely face scattered all over Kingston Pike.

A few months later, Jocelyn was scouted for a 1993 *Playboy* magazine spring campus batch edition. The photographer made her wear baby doll clothes. That was not her style. Jocelyn was a hippie at heart and liked to make her own clothes or borrow mine. Again, she changed her mind when she saw her naked photographs materialize and decided that was not the path she wanted to follow and definitely not how she wanted to be remembered.

Another eighth-floor Chattanooga tribe member, a freckled blonde named Cindy, stopped by our room often for a visit. The day after Cindy's boyfriend's car was broken into, she came over to tell the story to the half-dozen girls hanging out in our room. Her face progressively turned red, and she became more animated with every detail. Then she shouted, "Fucking [n-word]!"

I thought about all the Black people who had stood up for me throughout my life, a life that would have been cut a lot shorter had it not been for Mack Laramey and the real she-roes Bahija and the Tough Tanyas. I jumped off my bed, mirroring her rage within less than an inch from her face. "Don't you ever use that word!" I growled. Knowing Zelda was already dressed for battle and ready to make an appearance, I pointed toward the door and said, "You need to leave right now."

"I'm here to see Marnie, not you," she retorted.

I looked over at Marnie and said, "Hey, if you want to continue this conversation with your White-trash, piece-of-shit friend, you can do it in her room."

Cindy stormed out red-faced, and Marnie stayed put, saying nothing.

A few days later I went across the hall to visit Sloane and Jocelyn, who were suitemates with two very large Black girls who shared my love for the same scent at Victoria's Secret, Pear Glacé. They had a cork board in their foyer where I found a new photograph mixed in with their old collage, fastened with push pins. It was of Cindy smiling, altered by someone with a Sharpie who'd drawn a black swastika over her forehead. It gave me the creeps, as all Nazi paraphernalia does, but I took comfort in the fact that she did it to herself and that there were fewer people at UT to convince how wrong it was to use the n-word.

CHAPTER TWENTY-NINE

PASSOVER, BECAUSE THE WORLD NEEDS LESS NAZIS

Most of my friends from UT had never met or even seen a Jewish person, save for those on TV. Even then, they were often surprised by their Judaic heritage. Adam Sandler's "Hanukkah Song" came out when I was a freshman at UT, and it was very eye-opening for everyone. Julie flew down to Knoxville to come visit me for Passover weekend. I was still dating Greg.

We invited my roommates from Hellbourne, Jocelyn and Sloane, even though I wasn't actually living there. I spent most of my time at Greg's place, but I left my bed and some clothing items—such as the outfits I had splurged on from the Gap using the money I had earned working various jobs in high school—at Hellbourne. Jocelyn thought that by wearing my clothes and sleeping in my bed my confidence would rub off on her somehow. I enjoyed having someone think I was fashionable enough to want to wear my clothes.

Greg invited his friend, Jeremiah, who was a student at UT's veterinary school. Jeremiah had been working at his lab that day with some kind of red dye. I noticed a blood-like substance covering his hands and instructed him to wash before touching anything, but it was too late; there were already red fingerprints all over the door frame, and the joint that Greg had rolled. Julie and I declined it because we were unshowered and still in the midst of preparing food, and Jocelyn and Sloane were scheduled to arrive within the hour.

To prepare for Passover Seder, you must assemble the following items:

1. The Haggadah, the book that is read aloud, which we surprisingly found at a local Kroger, the only grocery store in Knoxville

2. A seder plate and accoutrements, which include a roasted egg to signify a new life after Egypt; bitter herbs as a nod to bitter times as slaves; matzah or unleavened bread, as there was no time to let it rise during the escape; parsley to render a new sign of life; charoset, a mix of apples, cinnamon, nuts, and wine representing the mortar used to make bricks as slaves; saltwater, for the tears; and a lamb bone, to depict the sacrifice on the last night

3. A candle

4. A glass of wine for Elijah, an honored spirit who slips in and takes a sip of wine when we aren't looking (we always assigned the role to my Uncle Ivan but figured Jeremiah would be the perfect substitute, once he washed his hands)

5. The food, which includes matzah ball soup, gefilte fish with red horseradish, and some kind of brisket, and for my family, due to my proclivity for my grandmother's cooking, noodle kugel for dessert (I didn't find out until my late thirties that noodles weren't really kosher for Passover; Mom Mom made it for me every visit because she knew how much I loved it, but she never had the heart to tell me)

Jules and I realized we'd forgotten to roast an egg for the seder plate! Time was running out, so we put one in the oven on broil. I removed it a few minutes later and set it out on the counter to cool right before I jumped in the shower. When I was in the finishing stages of my makeup application, I heard Julie scream, "What the hell!" I ran to the kitchen to see what was going on.

The egg, still hot and charred black from the broil setting of the oven, was billowing steam from one spot where a human bite had been taken, surrounded by red fingerprints. I looked at Jeremiah, who protested, "It wasn't me!" Jules and I both replied (in unison), "You've been caught red-handed!" and doubled over in laughter. The egg must have burned the shit out of his mouth. He didn't even bother to remove the shell.

We quickly assembled the seder plate with the half-eaten egg when Sloane and Jocelyn walked in the door. Everyone took their seat, and we began the Passover Seder. Julie assumed the role of "Master of the Table" because she was the only one who'd been bat mitzvahed, even though she was in high school at the time. When we came to the seder plate portion, which demonstrates the content's meaning, it dawned on us that we had neglected to buy a bitter herb. So we took a break to roll another joint as a substitute and I said, "Weed is an herb, right? Also, kind of bitter, I guess." We went around the room to give thanks . . . mostly to weed.

Every year I tell this story of how our version of Passover started in a shack in Knoxville, and each year the guest list continues to increase. Julie and I made a pledge to each other to continue to bring people together from different backgrounds and share the best parts of Judaism. We also wanted to make it fun, with lots of wine, to bring back that feeling of familial belonging we'd both experienced so long ago. To be specific, we made it mandatory for everyone to drink five glasses of red wine each, as we'd interpreted from our shortened (child's) version of the Haggadah, to make sure everyone had a good time.

Sharing is caring. We wanted my friends to have a rose-colored window into Judaism and to feel included. We made it an excuse to get together and throw a great party while sharing food and knowledge. This was just the beginning of my official quest to alleviate anti-Semitism in Knoxville with inclusivity, because the world needs less hatred and more love and understanding.

CHAPTER THIRTY

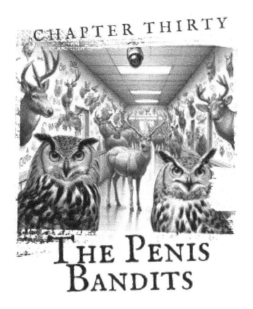

THE PENIS BANDITS

I met Kim at UT's orientation in front of the University Center. Twenty brand-new UT Volunteers sat in a circle, taking turns introducing ourselves. I said, "I'm from Reston, Virginia, located outside Washington, DC," so other rising freshmen understood the delineation. Northern Virginia is anything north of Manassas, which mostly consists of transplants from the Northeast, and the rest of Virginia is known for its countryside and predominantly Republican population.

We were supposed to take turns introducing ourselves by going clockwise, but Kim jumped the line and shouted out, "Me too! I went to Oakton!"

I found Kim to be slightly loud, clingy, and annoying at the time. Fast forward to a meet-and-greet at South Carrick dormitory with all the other eighth-floor residents, and the same exact thing happened. But this time, I clung back, happy to have a local ally so close. And just like that, we were attached at the hip, comforted by the familiarity of each other's way of speaking.

We both loved to poke fun at the news program *The Heartland Series*, which included feature stories about regional culture involving tanning hides, sawing logs, eating tree bark, carving soapstone, running a sawmill, making moonshine, calling a hoot owl, rutting like a deer, and knowing when the buffalo ran. We looked down from our high horse at the small-town mentality of the show, but we both also took issue with the general rampant racism of the South and agreed to enlist others to fight on our side.

Kim's roommate, Liza, whom we referred to as the "Queen of Sheeba" because of the way she piled her long, heavy, black hair on top of her head (also a term to describe anyone wearing a towel like a turban), stayed with her boyfriend for weeks at a time. It happened so often that I essentially moved into Kim's room, and Liza failed out of school. I lay in Liza's old bed for hours, listening to our favorite CDs such as *Shimmering, Warm & Bright* by Bel Canto and *The Angel in the House* by The Story.

Kim became my talent agent, convincing whoever was in control of the microphone to give it up for just one song, which was all I needed to woo an audience and obtain a round of free drinks. We were quite the diabolical duo. Jocelyn and Sloane made up a pejorative superlative for us: "Domineering Nasal Northern Women." I liked everything but the nasal part, mostly because of how much it rang true when I heard a recording of my voice playing back to me.

One time, we stayed up for 36 hours, simply because we never had. We wanted to discover what went on while everyone else was sleeping. We went to frat parties in the snow and stole random items such as candles, coasters, and church keys. We used fake IDs to get beer at the Circle K, where they took pictures of all their favorite patrons. (Circle K burned down due to arson during my sophomore year, but luckily we got the pictures before the store met its unfortunate end.) I also watched as green stripes appeared on my solid blue gloves. I knew the root of the hallucination was sleep deprivation. "I think it's time to hit the hay," I said, defeated.

The year 1994 was UT's bicentennial. Kim and I watched the activity in the courtyard through her dorm window. Kids played hacky sack and frisbee and congregated near the entrance to the food court. Our interest was piqued enough to get a closer look as we discovered folks setting up inside the food court for a talent contest, with the new UT football coach, Phil Fulmer, acting as the judge. They even made a stage with lighting and a sound box. I immediately entered and sang my go-to song by an artist Jocelyn had just introduced me to, Janice Joplin. My rendition of "Bobby McGee" rocked the house, and I won $100 and a certificate, handed to me by Coach Fulmer himself.

Kim accompanied me on trips back home, which were sometimes over eight hours with traffic and 16 hours in blizzard conditions. We loved making fun of Southerners and bonded over our Northernness. We noticed kudzu vines covering the trees like a blanket all over I-80. Thanks to *The Heartland Series*, we knew that kudzu is an invasive species brought over from Asia. It was initially brought to the US from Japan in 1876 as a way for farmers to prevent erosion, but it backfired big time. The net of kudzu strangled every sign of life along the drive from Knoxville to Northern Virginia. It was every-where, and just looking at it as we passed by caused a foreboding sense of claustrophobia.

I drove because Kim didn't have a car, which meant she was the default bowl packer. Kim passed the pipe over the console to me, still crackling, when I noticed red and blue lights flashing in my rear-view mirrors. Kim sprang into action by pouring a little Mountain Dew to extinguish the cherry and hiding the bowl under the seat. I pulled over, and the cop came around to Kim's side to ask us a series of questions.

Kim talked incessantly, as she did often, especially when she was anxious, which turned out to be a nifty technique to get out of tickets. After her soliloquy, she turned to me, still beaming nervously, but her smile was off. I immediately froze in fear, realizing her teeth

and lips were coated with black resin in the shape of an "O" from
our filthy bowl. She registered my flinch and shut her mouth. I did
the rest of the talking. Luckily, the cop gave us a warning and let us
go, with a reminder to stay under the speed limit. I handed Kim a
napkin and we laughed the rest of the way home.

I was always in a hurry to get where I was going; my anticipation
multiplied the weight of my lead foot, and like Danica Patrick driving
to Metallica's "Wherever I May Roam," the road became my bride.
Sometimes losing myself in thought was more amusing than the
destination, and I should have just enjoyed the reverie and the time
to reflect and hope for what was yet to come. But by the age of 20,
I'd racked up 16 consecutive speeding tickets with exorbitant fines,
and eventually a court-ordered traffic class for me and one lucky
(mandatory) parent.

My dad was such a good sport. He gave up his one day to golf,
his favorite reprieve from work, monotonous chores, and honey-do
lists, just to be stuck in a classroom all day with his delinquent daughter. I think he sensed how guilty I felt for fucking up all the time.
Also, we didn't get to spend much time alone with each other. So it
wasn't too terrible. Plus, now we both know not to switch lanes in an
intersection or drive over painted lines designated for parking spots.

Back at school, Kim, Jocelyn, Sloane, and I united and were brim-
ming with confidence. We changed all the words of the *Cheers* theme
song to, "Taking the break from the world today, takes everything
we've got. Looking good and smoking cigs, I wish we had some pot.
Would you like to know our names? Ellen, Kim, Sloane, Jocelyn!"

We'd shout out each of our names like you would scream "Salt!" from Jimmy Buffet's "Margaritaville."

We also marveled at the clever marketing skills from all the sororities on campus. Each member emblazoned their Greek letters on almost every article of clothing, including sweatshirts, jackets, sweatpants, hair ribbons, and sneakers, like the *Saturday Night Live* skit "Delta Delta Delta, can I help ya help ya help ya?" Posters were plastered all over our dorm, even though sororities already had an entire Panhellenic Building for themselves, which had been built in 1963.

The posters infiltrating our dorm were beautifully handwritten and had colorfully illustrated artwork that must have taken hours to create. They were adorable, but Sloane, Jocelyn, Kim, and I wanted to punish sororities for being exclusive, rich, and entitled. So we gathered in disguise weekly to deface and destroy the posters, alternating nights as a diversion tactic. We made up old man names for each us, to use as code to communicate with each other during the mission. I was Carl, Kim was Stanley, Sloane was Ronald, and Jocelyn was Chester. We put rolls of toilet paper under our sweat suits to camouflage our body shapes and pantyhose over our faces, and like Quentin Tarantino's *Reservoir Dogs*, we were all assigned colored markers. I was Mr. Brown.

We traveled by the stairwell, split up into two groups to cover both sides quickly, and drew giant hairy dicks on each and every poster. Farm animals were our favorite, and there were plenty. We appointed the right wing's eighth-floor stairwell to discard our camouflage in the event we were chased but never needed to use it. The resident advisors coined the term "Penis Bandits" and tried to catch us by installing security cameras, which we discovered and worked around. No one ever caught us, and I just broke a 30-year vow of silence, but I guess the dicks are out of the bag now.

CHAPTER THIRTY-ONE

CROSS PHOBIA

I have a visceral response to the advertisement of religion. Does God care what you wear? To me, a crucifix is a reminder of a very gory and morbid scene predating 22 centuries of holy wars and colonization, systemically rooted in white supremacy. I detest the fearmongering behind the Christian heaven-and-hell narrative. However, I've been able to curb my judgment in recent years by understanding the inclination to procure and keep a talisman on your person.

At UT, bible beaters stood in my path on my way to class weekly, handing out religious pamphlets and asking, "Will you accept Jesus Christ as your savior?" or something similarly mawkish. My reply was always, "Wrong girl" or "Sir, you'll need to recalibrate your Jew-dar; it doesn't appear to be working." My all-time favorite was, "No, thanks. When I read, I prefer nonfiction." Usually that did the trick, save for the psycho, sexist, tyrannical street preacher.

On my way to my critical thinking philosophy class, which I had to take to satisfy a math requirement without actually having to take math, a loud, angry man hurled insults at all the women walking by the corner of Frances St. and Andy Holt Ave. He wore a tattered burlap dress and carried a six-foot wooden cross made of 4 x 4-inch boards. A woman I assumed was his wife stood next to him, along with five or six female children who were all wearing white night-gowns and barefoot, looking absolutely miserable. They were like the cult members of the Guilty Remnant from *The Leftovers*, except dirty and neglected.

"Women should be at home caring for children, preparing food and doing housework, not homework, whoring after a man's knowledge!" he screamed. I wished someone would just punch him in his loud mouth, but I had the compunction to ignore him because I needed to get to class. Once there, I found a note on the door that read, "Class canceled due to illness." It was a sign. From whom I didn't know, but I had to turn around and confront the verbally abusive street zealot.

A crowd had gathered. The nutball was shouting at a teacher, "Your job is filthy devil's work, woman!"

I stepped in and said, "Speaking of filth, where the fuck are these kids' shoes and why aren't they in school?"

He raised his voice into a shrill. "Spawn of the devil! Pig! Whore!"

And that was it. Never call a Jewish person a pig. It's not kosher (pun intended). I turned to the crowd to address them and shouted, "Did you all hear that?"

Everyone confirmed receipt. "Yes!" they shouted.

My showmanship in full force, I put up my fists for emphasis. "And do you think this slander of the innocent warrants physical retaliation?"

The crowd cheered and clapped. "YES! Do it! Punch him in the dick!" they shouted.

I turned back to the man and smiled, mimicking his maniacal expression. Remembering my lessons from Bahija and Zach—"Stun with your left for accuracy, then punch with the right for power"—I aimed for the back of the man's head for good follow-through. I felt the skin and bones of his face envelop my knuckles upon contact. The first hit stupefied him, the second knocked him stumbling backward. He pulled his cross down with him. I picked up the bottom and started to run it in circles, forcing him to spin in smaller circles from the ground.

The crowd went wild, but the police appeared suddenly. They had been waiting in the wings and decided to intervene. They pulled me down a flight of stairs, handcuffed me, and gently guided me into the back of their vehicle.

A woman the man had been harassing earlier approached the cops. Whatever she said was highly effective, as I was immediately released from the car and exonerated from the assault. She handed me her card and said, "Call in the morning if you have any more problems." I glanced at her title: a UT administrator. I figured she was the one who called the cops and together we were responsible for scaring the demented man off campus for good. There were others who took his place, I'm sure. Knoxville is still considered the Bible Belt for a reason.

Later, someone put up a poster at the site of the incident that read, "Jesus, Moses, and Muhammad want us to get along." Kim took a picture while I held up a peace sign with my fingers. We knew the poster had been addressed and written directly to me. I must have taken the poster to heart, for this was my last brush with the law over violence. I didn't want to go to jail for assault and battery. My fighting career was over, and my future was free from any further criminal activity.

As summer drew close and my savings ran out, I needed to get a job. My dad and I argued a lot about who should pay for what, and I didn't have enough money for the basics, like beer and weed. Greg and I broke up when he came home tripping on acid. "Your aura is purple," he said. "What does that mean?" I asked. But he couldn't explain, and the next day he dropped out of engineering. The stray cat he'd been taking care of had shat on his waterbed and escaped through the window. It was time for me to go as well.

At home, L&N Seafood had an opening for a server. I'd waited tables before at Fuddruckers in Herndon, Virginia, where they'd strung cow carcasses from their hind legs, suspended by their hooves in a floor-to-ceiling window, right next to the cashier line. Back then, I relied on my friend Samantha to take me to work, so we always needed to take the same shifts. Fuddruckers introduced me to the song "Hey Jude" by the Beatles, which always played while I vacuumed the intricate carpet. Unfortunately, one month into the job, Samantha got a DUI and we both were forced to quit.

When I got my own car, I worked as a hostess at a place in Herndon called the Texas Crab. In Knoxville, I worked at O'Charley's, Olive Garden, and Macaroni Grill. After all those restaurants, you'd think I'd perfected the art of waiting tables, but I was never any good. I ran out of patience for people who didn't ask for everything they wanted while ordering, and I couldn't hide my frustration when someone asked for extras such as mustard or a fork. Sometimes patrons neglected to tip me, and I'd often get saddled with a bill from folks playing dine-and-dash. I thought, *Maybe in Reston things will be different? Also, Ellen from L&N sure has a nice ring to it!*

My training at L&N Seafood, otherwise known as shadowing, paid $2 per hour and was supposed to last four days. Only then would I have the freedom to wait tables on my own. My trainer was a loud, mediocre, White male in his mid twenties who covered the process of "the upcharge" on day two. He said, "When patrons ask for substitutions, don't let them Jew you down."

I was shocked. First, I thought everyone could tell I was Jewish, and second, I'd never heard that term before. He acted as though it was common nomenclature. My blood began to boil, but I channeled my anger management coach, who had instructed me to turn around in situations where I could only see red; to keep Zelda at bay. Well, I *tried* to channel my anger management coach. Instead, I yelled, "Go fuck yourself, you loudmouthed bigot!" and threw my apron at him and walked out the door. At least I didn't hit him.

CHAPTER THIRTY-TWO

THE MAMMOTH MISTAKE

My friend Jason was from Mt. Airy, Maryland, the same town where the brother camp to Camp Louise was located. Jason was one of nine kids from a very Catholic family, so he'd never been to Camp Airy. He had blond hair, blue eyes, and a sharp, cutting wit that made me laugh and fear his mockery in equal measure. We were both psych majors and had always been close in a platonic way, but over two years we'd developed feelings for each other, starting when he held my hand to walk me down to the field at Neyland Stadium. I was performing with the UT's Pride of the Southland half-time show. We sang a jazz medley with the marching band to "Paper Moon." For all the non-football-caring folks like me, this was the year Heath Shuler was quarterback, one year before the arrival of Peyton Manning.

Prior to our romantic relationship, Jason let me borrow his car to go home for a funeral when one of my Chantilly High School friends committed suicide. I drove all night and was taking a nap when my sister swiped the keys and drove the car into a parked vehicle outside Mom's condo unit. Julie freaked out and lost control when she saw our stepdad arriving home. Someone called the cops, and I was ordered, by both my parents, to take the fall. Julie was fifteen and didn't have a license. I missed the funeral service, and the damage was $650. From what little I remember, Jason's insurance claimed it to be a hit-and-run and incurred the monthly cost increase.

Jason and I loved each other, but we weren't really "in love." We had fun exploring Knoxville and made a good team of like-minded Northerners, until I did something really stupid: I stopped taking birth control because someone, I actually think it was my doctor, told me I should take breaks to ensure I wasn't causing long-term effects on my fertility. Julie was graduating from South Lakes when I realized my period was late. I went home for the ceremony and simultaneously confirmed a positive pregnancy test with my gyne-cologist. The minute the test came back, I begged my doctor to eliminate the pregnancy. I'd already learned about RU-486 in school. Unfortunately, it wasn't FDA-approved until September of 2000, which was another four years away.

I just wanted to take care of my situation as quickly as possible. I had way too much to accomplish to get stuck in a parent trap with no money, no husband, no degree, and a brain in need of a few more years to fully develop. Jason left the choice up to me but was also incredibly immature and irresponsible. His parents stopped paying his tuition, and he was "auditing" all his classes, hoping to pay the bills from a side gig as a sous chef. I knew I wanted to get married and have a family someday, but not with him. I wanted a man to fall in love with the woman version of me (I didn't feel like a woman just yet) and on their own terms, not because they felt forced to do "the right thing." Moreover, I didn't want to bring an unwanted child into the world.

My dad's insurance company told him to schedule an appoint-ment with Planned Parenthood, but as soon as my father and I walked in the door, I knew something was seriously wrong. There were baby pictures lining the walls and happy couples seated in the lobby. Someone called my name and brought us into an office. A woman sitting at the desk facing us said, "You and your partner can take a seat."

I was horrified. "This is my dad!" I exclaimed. "Where are the operating tables and doctors?"

The woman told me to calm down and that I was there to discuss my options. We left nauseated and disgusted.

Soon after, I directly called an abortion clinic in Falls Church, Virginia, to make sure it wasn't another bait-and-switch. This time, my mom drove me. Protestors stationed in the parking lot holding pro-life signs and jars with contents resembling fetuses blocked our way to the door. These people were demented; they screamed and chased everyone entering the building. With no one to protect us from the bat-shit-crazy mob, Mom dropped me off around the back and parked across the street.

Once inside, I noticed an older woman sitting next to me who was wearing a substantial diamond on her ring finger. I wondered what her story was, but of course, said nothing. Across the room was a little girl who couldn't be older than 13, crying softly next to three or four other women of various ages and races. We all wore the same forlorn expressions. They called my name and took me into a lab to collect my blood.

The nurse asked me a list of questions to distract me from the needle. The light in the corners of my vision started to fade like a vignette filter. When I came to, I was still sitting in the chair.

"Ellen, are you okay?" Mom asked.

"Wow, I'm really lightheaded," I said. I was so nervous I must have passed out from holding my breath.

Next stop, the operating room. Once again, I lost all possible semblance of composure when the anesthesiologist came into the room. My dad's family has a history of a hereditary disorder called pseudocholinesterase deficiency, a worst-nightmare reaction to anesthetic that causes paralysis, an inability to breathe or talk, yet keeps the person conscious while going under the knife. Luckily, I was spared from this additional trauma by use of general anesthesia as opposed to succinylcholine. The cost to put me out was an extra $300, bringing the total up to an eerily familiar $650. Some of the women chose to remain conscious to avoid the cost; others did it to punish themselves.

When I woke up, I was surrounded by the ladies from the lobby and still groggy from the procedure. We were all crying. We sat in big leather chairs with pads covering them. I was wearing a giant maxi pad and could feel the warmth of blood seeping out from the operation.

I bled for days and was severely depressed for three full months, the remainder of the summer break. Everything about it was miserable, but I'm so thankful for Falls Church Reproductive Health Center. Without it, I would have had to sacrifice everything—my dreams, my career, a marriage of love versus one of duty, and the type of relationship I wanted with my parents, independent versus codependent.

I don't regret the decision; I just wish I'd been smarter. Also, I didn't realize how physically, mentally, and politically traumatic the process would be. Thinking I was going to Planned Parenthood only to end up in a waiting room full of happy expecting mothers and fathers was only the beginning of the trauma. To then have a counselor mistakenly think my dad was the father was horrifying and makes me sick even to this day. Overall, the fake clinic, the clinical detachment of the planned parenthood staff, the political tension surrounding abortion, and my subsequent months-long depression (a normal chemical reaction that happens when a woman loses a fertilized egg) culminated in an extremely difficult time.

A few years later, when I was living in NYC, Jason showed up at my door for a surprise visit. I still have no idea how he found me. I wasn't feeling well and told him I'd bring him to a happy hour with a few friends from work, but then I needed to go home and get some sleep. Jason didn't have a job and had been couch surfing for the better part of two years. He never graduated.

I stayed for 30 minutes at happy hour, then left him there with my friend Marylin. I was exhausted and fell asleep as soon as my head hit the pillow of my junior one-bedroom apartment. Sometime around midnight, the buzzer rang. Jason and Marylin were as drunk as skunks. I buzzed them in, knowing how far away Marylin lived with her parents in Queens and that Jason had nowhere else to go. Thirty minutes after settling down on the futon, Marylin woke up to puke all over Jason, my comforter, and the futon. I told Jason to clean it up and figure it out. He wiped up the vomit with a towel and threw it onto the fire escape, along with my comforter. They went back to sleep with only a sheet and each other to keep warm. The next day, I found the towel and the blanket in a heap near the trash cans and told Jason to lose my number, forever. Marylin apologized profusely and I immediately forgave her.

Years later, when I interviewed Jocelyn for this book, she told me that Jason had stolen one of her topless "light testing" polaroids from the *Playboy* shoot. She knew one of them went missing after Jason had been over to our house and was able to confirm this from a friend of her boyfriend's. They had seen the picture when Jason passed it around to his entire dorm floor, reveling in schadenfreude. What a piece of shit.

I can't imagine what my life would have been like had I not terminated that pregnancy. It was a difficult decision, and one I did not take lightly. I don't know where Jason is or what he's up to now, but even then I had the foresight to know that neither he nor I was ready for the immense responsibility that having a child brings. I had screwed up so many things in my young life, and I knew that making that decision would prevent me from screwing things up again.

CHAPTER THIRTY-THREE

THE AMBER WAVES OF PEYTON MANNING

Life is only what we make of it. To sum up my experience at UT, I tried everything and leveraged every opportunity that came my way.

I declared a minor in vocal performance, but the music credit system at UT was bullshit, requiring four classes/practices per week for performances along with Friday night rehearsals and Saturday performances once a month. Yet we received only one credit per semester, whereas every other class gave credit for the total hours of participation, per week.

Music theory is basically another version of math using a staff instead of a calculator, making music impossible for me at times. But a nice consolation was a very handsome, blond music lit teacher who played music in class to help us understand the concepts while they permeated our ears; for example, the term "dissonance." He played "The Rite of Spring" by Stravinsky and showed us how to bang our hands on the desk to capture the spasmodic rhythm of the song. "The Rite of Spring," with its jerky, irregular beat, was so displeasing to the ear it caused a riot in Paris on May 29, 1913. Outraged audience members drowned out the orchestra as they hurled objects at the stage, started fights, and were arrested. It was a fantastic song!

I had a hard time keeping up. The class materials included a book called *Listen* by Joseph Kerman and six CDs with 20 to 30 songs on each. We were expected to memorize and recite each song's era (medieval, renaissance, baroque, romantic, or modern), form (fugue, sonata, minuet, rondo, concerto), genre (Gregorian chant, madrigal, symphony, opera), and time or key signature. Retention was very time-consuming, which made me question my choice to follow this musical path to nowhere.

Most of the music majors were intense and overbearing, except for one guitar player named Brock, who took an interest in me as a vocalist. Brock's exotically long, shiny, dark hair fell to the middle of his back, and his small, angular face was handsome. At first, I figured he just wanted to date me, but after several trips to his home to listen to all the mixed tapes of women he'd made for me because he wanted me to imitate them, I realized he wanted to keep things professional and how profoundly serious he was about the business of music.

I already had Sinéad O'Connor, Bjork, and Natalie Merchant pretty close to perfection, but Brock wanted me to experiment to find the full expanse of my own voice and the mastery of using it with finesse. He played Mazzy Star and said, "Doesn't it sound like her voice is coming from the inside of a jar?" She must have liked the concert hall reverb setting on the sound board, just like me. However, I found Sinéad's voice to be the most cavernous, just as Anita Baker assesses her in Sinéad's memoir *Rememberings: Scenes from My Complicated Life.*

In the '90s, information was communicated through flyers on bulletin boards outside of class. I responded to a band searching for a lead singer who could write lyrics and went to an audition held in the drummer's grandparents' garage. To get to the makeshift practice space, we had to walk through the house, and then through the overgrown, mosquito-infested garden in the backyard. The garage had wood paneling on the walls and strange things in boxes, such as fake swords and shields and Monty Python costumes.

They offered me the lead singer job on the spot. We decided on the name "Yellow #5" because there were five of us, yellow was our favorite color, and we liked the things with the ingredient yellow #5—Twinkies and Mountain Dew. Also, Maroon 5 hadn't made it yet.

Our setlist was 13 original songs, one of which was named "Zelda":

Zelda
Once there was a little girl named Zelda
She had a problem with sitting still each day
Her folks tried therapy to calm her
But the drugs only made her stay awake

Zelda got into an ugly fight,
another day she called the teacher nasty names
Suspensions, expulsions for belligerence
Zelda knew she'd played the last of her games

Still not right, she couldn't sleep,
so she took some antihistamines to help her dream
They made her feel kind of woozy, like her body was all juicy
So they sent her away, they sent her away

At night toss and turn, hoping that she might learn
A way to sleep, a way to sleep and help her dream

(Zelda is a star, Zelda is a star)
Poor Zelda . . . Nowhere to call home

The Zelda of my youth was starting to fade, but it was fun to bring her back to life in song. We played in venues including McGee's Irish Pub, The Mercury Theater, The Lap and Library, and a new brew pub downtown. We even made it into the Knoxville news when we were shopping our demo to local bars to get gigs. The piece was about a kid who had been overserved in a bar, and we were asked our thoughts. I said, "Oh, I wish someone had cut me off the night I drank myself into an alcohol-poisoned nightmare." Hindsight is 20/20.

Peyton Manning was the second out of three UT quarterbacks when I was there. We were in a medieval studies class together, which was popular among many football players. When I worked at the UT library, many of his football comrades would frequent it. Whether they were simply coming for tutoring or just thought I was cute, I will never know. Peyton never accompanied his teammates to the library, but I did see him once at Hawkeyes, where I sang Bonnie Raitt's version of "Angel from Montgomery" with the band. He stood near the exit, along with several other classmates. He gave me a thumbs up among the applause. When I walked off the stage, my boyfriend made a beeline to intercept me with a hug. I paused to show loyalty but kept my eyes glued to the back of the room and pushed forward to greet the group of gargantuan boys. Peyton said, "Wow, I didn't know you could sing. You were great." I said, "Thanks," and smiled like I had won the lottery.

The most Yellow #5 earned was a whopping $1,000 performing for a frat/sorority mixer at a bar called Bonkers which was also the night I kicked a glass of champagne all over my monitor and my band told me to "slow down." At the pre-party, I snorted what was supposed to be 'pure Colombian' cocaine with my boss from the library. During intermission, someone passed me a joint in the hallway near the bathrooms. My guitarist, Pete, looked over at my drummer, Brad, and remarked, 'We are getting into 911 territory.' I must have overheard it. Instead of trying to reassure them, I bared my teeth and growled. The set list was cut in half, and the bar attempted to halve our fee as well. We entered a contest called the Battle of the Bands. I'm not sure how many bands auditioned, but we were one of five and the only band with a female (me). We placed fourth and decided we were robbed, or the world just wasn't ready for Yellow #5 yet.

I enjoyed every minute spent with these kind, talented, and sweet gentlemen who were always so encouraging. Brad and Pete were in graduate school and very mature. I was only 21, so they cut me some slack about the night I got really out of control. Even their lovely girlfriends would come to the show and mouth all the lyrics I wrote right along with me as I sang them. I've stayed in touch with them, all except our bassist Tony, who died of alcoholism. Rock and Roll is indeed a dangerous business. However, Brad and Pete would eventually go on to earn their PhD's. And Justin, the rhythm guitarist, is now an award winning journalist overseas. I think Robin Williams summed it up it best when he said "Cocaine – paranoid and impotent, what fun. Useless conversations until midnight, waking up at dawn feeling like a vampire on a day pass. No". I only experimented with it a few more times before realizing rock stardom wasn't meant for me.

Over Christmas break, I had to get my wisdom teeth extracted. Dad had moved to Pennsylvania for work, so there was nowhere for me to go home to except for Mom's. Dad's dental insurer was just as bad at referrals as his medical insurer; they sent me to a butcher. I had bruises all over my arm from where they stabbed me repeatedly with needles, and I woke up spitting up pieces of bone. Julie fed me Vicodin like candy, and Mom took a picture of me looking like a chipmunk with a mouth full of nuts and framed it.

Back at school, I developed two dry sockets and a subsequent infection. Mom came to UT for a visit and went to my classes for me. She took fantastic notes and got to meet Peyton Manning, and my favorite professors: Dr. Moses, from medieval studies and Dr. Renee Repka, from Human Sexuality and Abnormal Psych. I started feeling better the second day of Mom's trip and took her to the UT library to show her the periodicals department where I worked.

I snuck her up to the staff balcony on the top floor. The entrance had a metal keypad that required a code. I dialed the numbers, shielding her view. "Employees only," I joked. Outside, the sun was just setting behind the clouds on the horizon. The sky was an endless canvas of a perfectly fitting Tennessee Orange hue. This was the best view of the campus and Neyland Stadium. As we stood near the railing, taking in the cityscape, the Tennessee river sparkled in shades of topaz and amber, reflecting the sky. I thanked my mother for believing in me, encouraging me to come back to college, and not giving up on us.

CHAPTER THIRTY-FOUR

SCARFACE AT McGEE'S IRISH PUB

During freshman year I'd met a group of fellow female Northerners and started UT's first club field hockey team with them. We traveled to places such as Virginia Tech and Vanderbilt. At first we enlisted only women and had an older local female coach from South Africa. But once we lost badly to a coed team, we decided to recruit males. The team bonded by binge-drinking after every practice, and we became so close that we even spent spring break together in Florida.

In my late twenties, I ran into Coach Wellchase at the Safeway grocery store in at South Lakes shopping center. I thought about confronting her to say something like, "Hey, Coach, guess what? I started the very first field hockey team in history at UT, and we went varsity my senior year. Sounds like you made a big mistake! Big! HUGE!" But I just couldn't muster the nerve. Despite all my anger management training, I worried I'd lose my cool and cause a scene. Also, the South Lakes Safeway was the closest grocery store to my house, and I couldn't risk getting arrested there.

After initially living in the dorms, I branched out in my living situation. Lainey was a friend from field hockey, a fellow Northerner, and we decided to search for a house with acquaintances of our New England captain, Tammy – a girl and two gentlemen named Cheri, Dave, and Joey. This was to circumvent an antiquated brothel law (possibly legend) that Knoxville had at the time, which prohibited more than four girls living together. We found a neglected, dilapidated, five-bedroom house with wood floors and a broken front door, which ended up being my bedroom door. The window in the door had black electrical tape in the shape of a spiderweb to keep the shattered glass in place and a towel stuffed into the three-inch gap at the bottom to keep the vermin out. The house had been built in 1905 and looked as though it had been through several fires. Black soot laced the surface of the red bricks, giving the house a hazardous, "should've been condemned years ago" look.

Cheri, a blue-eyed brunette with curly hair, hailed from Connecticut, while Lainey, also of Italian descent, had green eyes and curly blonde hair, originating from North East, Maryland. I made minimum wage at my library job, Lainey worked as a nanny, and Cheri was a server at Copper Cellar, which used to be the most upscale fancy restaurant in Knoxville. Lainey and Cheri taught me how to throw a noodle on the wall or bite into it to see whether it was cooked. If it was white on the inside or it fell off the wall, it wasn't done. They also taught me how to cook alfredo sauce from scratch with three simple ingredients: milk, parmesan, and butter.

Joel, the landlord, looked like an alcoholic lion and was a very poor repairman, but the rent was cheap. The house included a 70-year-old wayfarer named Bob who lived in the basement and would have been homeless if it hadn't been for Joel, who helped Bob earn his living by collecting parking fees in our backyard during football games.

When our cable went out, Lainey learned how to use a coax cable splitter and needed to get into the basement. Bob opened the door to reveal an appallingly wretched slum. His food was hanging in cereal boxes from a string of twine stretched across the ceiling made of 2 x 4s and plywood. His bed was just a sleeping bag on a cushion in the corner of the floor made of dirt. Now we understood why Bob took his showers outside, fully clothed in an ensemble of blue coveralls he wore every day. The backyard charge of $10 per car was likely his only income. When I asked Lainey what she remembers about our time at 400 12'h Street, she said, "I still can't believe we had a homeless man living in our basement!"

I struck gold when I discovered a new musical therapist in Ani DiFranco's *Living in Clip* album. My friend Laith from my music classes was playing bass to accompany his girlfriend singing "Untouchable Face," the most beautifully honest song I'd ever heard. I played it on repeat, which drove everyone in the house absolutely nuts. I also wore out Fleetwood Mac's *Greatest Hits*, the *Evita* soundtrack, and bootlegs from Dave Matthews, but at least I listened during waking hours.

During the week of finals, the boys had an impromptu party upstairs. Their speakers were the size of two standard refrigerators. I'd been studying for hours and just wanted to go to sleep. At 1 a.m., I went up the stairs and told everyone to be quiet, but the music was being controlled from inside Dave's bedroom, where he and the field hockey team's captain, Tammy, were getting it on. I barged in to turn off the subwoofers, and we all had a standoff, two against one. They were not happy with the interruption and retaliated by turning up the bass even more. I went downstairs and counter-retaliated by summoning the police via a noise complaint and left to sleep at my boyfriend's apartment. How times had changed. When I was in high school, any sign of cops most likely meant I'd gotten into some kind of trouble. Now I was calling the cops on my roommates!

By my super senior year, I'd been through three rounds of roommates. My last two were the worst! They were notorious for contributing nothing and stealing everything. I guess this was the short end of karma for me. I ended up putting a lock on my door and was forced to hide my shampoo and razors, leaving only one bar of soap behind in the shower, which my last roommate, Krissy, used to wash her body and hair. I found the inconvenient solution of just carrying a shower caddy around. One day, Krissy showed up at the local cafe where she worked, barefoot. When her manager asked what happened to her shoes, she said, "God took them." I wonder whether she thought that's what happened to all the soap.

Our club field hockey team went varsity the year I graduated, 1998. The only team I remember beating us (after going coed) was the Atlanta women's field hockey team, my very last game, when a foul ball necessitated eight stitches under my left eye. I was super hungover, and it was raining buckets. I tried my best to get out of that last dingleberry of a game. We'd already won every game in the tournament, and the whole team was confident the last one would be canceled due to rain, which makes for a dangerous sport. But Tammy was relentless, pestering and browbeating the shit out of me to get out of bed and onto the fields. I had everyone's stick in my trunk and we'd all tied one on to celebrate the wins. I think I was still drunk enough to believe I could muster up some energy, but I should have told her to fuck off.

Too tired and slow to get out of the way, I watched the foul ball hurtling toward my face in what felt like slow motion. When it hit, the pain was unbearable. I dropped to the ground instantly. The team surrounded me as I clutched my face in agony.

"Let me see it," Tammy said.

I stood up and removed my hands from my aching cheek and eye. I saw a flash of concern rush across her face.

"Oh, it's just a little blood," she said.

I didn't realize the ball had broken my skin, and I went into full-on panic mode. "I knew it!" I yelled. "I told you this would happen!!" To this day, I blame her. J'accuse!

My Irish friend and teammate Caitriona drove my car to the hospital, where they applied Lidocaine on my wound. The doctor said it was part "cocaine," then clarified' "It's just a local anesthetic so you won't feel the needle stabs when I administer your stitches." He added, "By the way, you're lucky you didn't break the orbit of your eye."

The mangled laceration and my black eye got worse over time, turning brown and yellow before disappearing. With only one week left before graduation, I wore my UT field hockey sweatshirt every day so that people didn't think I'd lost a fight. After the whole team signed it, I donated my jersey to the Irish Pub where Caitriona worked and received my very first, and might I say, very inventive, nickname: Scarface.

I met Caitriona in acting class, where I learned how to put on makeup in front of an audience and to change my gait by shifting the center of balance from my knees to my rib cage so that I could walk like Lainey, my favorite person to imitate. It gave me an excuse to swish my butt back and forth. We practiced our characters, walking around a mirrored room lined with ballet bars.

Caitriona taught me everything I know about Irish culture, where everything is either "shyte" or "brilliant" and everyone is an "eejit." She arrived at UT on a full scholarship for tennis but was wearing a sling around her arm and could no longer play, having just blown her shoulder out. I invited her to play field hockey with us and she became our star player. I had found my calling in the field of recruiting earlier than I thought.

Our team's favorite place to drink was at McGee's Irish Pub on the strip in Knoxville, where Caitriona was a bartender. The rustic bar had a piano where I played "Lean on Me" and everyone sang along. Caitriona told everyone about the soldiers who drank Guinness stout to replace meals during war and who refused to drink it unless the "right" method of pouring was administered, and she insisted that we should never try it in bottle form. She could pound a pint of Guinness in less than three seconds. Nobody could outdrink her, not even the biggest, burliest rugby players that frequented McGee's. "How in the world did you do that?" I'd ask. "Just open your troat," she'd say while drawing shamrocks in the foamy head of her beer. She also told me that Irish people can't make the "th" sound. They even have a nursery rhyme: "Dis, Dat, Dees, and Does, Dat's de Way de 'T.H.' Goes."

Caitriona taught me how Irish people had been oppressed by the British for centuries, how Gaelic, Ireland's indigenous language, wasn't allowed to be spoken for over eight hundred years, and how to say things like "kiss my ass" (*Póg mo thóin*, pronounced "poag-ma-hone") and "shut your mouth" (*dún do bhéal*, pronounced "dune-de-vail"). The most forbidden was the Irish Republican Army's slogan *tiocfaidh ár lá* (pronounced "chuckie-ar-la"), which translates to "our day will come." She told me to never say it in front of a Protestant unless I wanted to get my ass kicked.

Though Caitriona was fascinating and very sweet, she was also extremely competitive. She eviscerated her opponents in everything. I was enamored by her skill and charmed by her accent, but it was actually her dry, cerebral sense of humor that I found most enchanting. Caitriona picked up the pieces after one of a million breakups with Ricky, the boy who had just broken my heart. She posted his picture on our dart board and got the whole house involved. Everyone took turns throwing darts through his beautiful face, insisting I deserved better, while hitting the target perfectly in the middle. "Bullseye!" she said and flashed me a smile. I knew we'd be friends for life.

CHAPTER THIRTY-FIVE

THE TROUBLEMAKER'S UNDERWEAR

For my second cousin's wedding in Bowie, Maryland, I didn't have enough money to buy a nice formal dress. It was August, so I got away with wearing a sundress I found at a store called Rave in a strip mall in Knoxville. It was in my favorite yellow gingham print (Rachael Checkers) and was only $4. The fabric was rayon . . . or chiffon . . . . I have no idea because I know nothing about fabrics. I couldn't afford most things, including food, and my lean frame became more gawky and flat-chested as a result. I didn't even need to wear a bra with the dress, just adhesive bandages for my nipples and a white cotton thong panty. I looked in the full-length mirror in the hotel room where my family had gathered and thought I looked like hot shit! The telephone rang, and my hilarious cousin Brad answered: "Bowie Morgue, how can I help you?"

My cousin Naomi was marrying a rabbi named Noah, who was new to our tradition of photo taking: first lining up by age, then by height. My poor cousin-in-law Leigh is always the shortest and old-est, but such a wonderful sport and the sharpest knife in the family drawer. Noah was visibly overwhelmed by our big personalities but smiled for the camera with the grace of a public speaker. Naomi looked beautiful. Her white beaded dress sparkled in the light shining through the hallway windows. She looked like an angel. I went in for a hug, and her mother, Loretta, grabbed the glass of white wine out of my hand and said, "No liquids near the dress, hon."

A few weeks later an envelope arrived in the mail from Naomi and Noah, which I assumed was a thank-you note for the card that Julie had written and added my name to out of kindness. To my surprise, it was a photograph of our cousin lineup, with lighting so effective it gave the camera an X-ray quality. The picture had been widely distributed to every family member, which was unfortunate for me since the lines of my white thong were so pronounced that I might as well have been wearing a dress made of cellophane. I started getting calls from my cousins all over the country. "Hello?" I'd answer. "Nice tighty-whities, coz," they'd say, then laugh non-stop, so intensely I could almost see them collapsing to the floor and rolling around. Julie framed the picture and displayed it prominently in her home.

My mom didn't share the details of her past with me, so I was left to make my own assumptions when her sisters kept calling to weasel their way back into our lives through me. It frustrated them when I didn't have answers. I begged them to call my mom instead and encouraged them to work out their problems so we could get back to being a family, but it never happened.

As a little kid, I thought that because Bugger, Aunt Ro, and Aunt Patsy were my family, it meant they were obligated to love me. When Mom couldn't show up for me because of work, her family stood in for her. I was the first person on my mom's side to go to college. So when Mom wouldn't allow any of her family to attend my graduation, I thought I was being penalized.

As time went on, Mom shared bits of information to help me understand the bigger picture. The family breakup wasn't about me. Mom excluded the family from my graduation because it was the easiest way to sever ties for good. Once she processed what happened during her childhood, out on that balcony, and continued to "do the work" through my college years, she was finally able to move on and let go of the anger, pain, and sorrow she'd been carrying throughout her life. She didn't want to share my success with the family, knowing how easy it would be for them to ruin her joy with one nasty remark, a risk she wasn't willing to take.

The day of graduation, I stood on the court of UT's Thompson Boling Arena and looked up at the stands, where 20,000 family members sat. I thought about how much better the world would be if all the crusty old bigots died, save for my own (and any other) nonracist, human rights activist grandparents. At that exact moment, those same grandparents were asking my dad to double-check the program for my name to make sure I was actually graduating. Luckily, they found it, and I received a Bachelor of Arts within the hour.

That degree remains one of my most treasured and cherished possessions—not just for the date of 1998, the year UT won the national championship in football for the sixth time in history, but for the achievement I came so close to giving up on multiple times, mostly because of all the time I spent doubting myself instead of learning how to . . . well, learn. It took me two years to figure out how to take good notes, read the specific parts of books I would eventually be tested on, get organized, and do the work to mentally absorb the information.

After the ceremony, Mom Mom and Pop Pop took me, Dad, LeeAnn, Brandon, Julie, and my boyfriend Ricky out for dinner at a fancy seafood restaurant. I had earned myself a spot on the Dean's List each of my last four semesters. They were all so proud of me! I gave credit to my job at the library, a place where I could study as well as correspond with loved ones over email, a place where I gained the ability to communicate efficiently (and finally legibly). I also thanked Ricky's engineering lab that allowed me to study alongside him, since that's where he spent 95 percent of his time. Pop Pop and Ricky discovered they were both in the same engineering fraternity, Theta Tau. I made a mental note that engineers make good boyfriends and husbands.

When the meal was over, I asked the server for a box to bring home all the free leftover bread. Dad was embarrassed, just like he was when my grandparents drove past my house on 12th street. "How could you let her live there, Jeffrey?" Mom Mom said. I didn't care that I lived in a dump. I didn't care that I was taking leftover bread to go. I had just graduated from college. Five years before that, I had been kicked out of my high school. I had fought my way through school, working hard and bettering myself, and no one was going to diminish that gift I had given myself.

Mom's Prom,
1967

1976

Dad, College

Wedding,
1973

Mom &
Dad

My Favorite Rocking Chair

Top left to right: Aunt Ro, Mom, Aunt Eileen Bottom: Aunt Caroline, Bugger, Aunt Patsy

Hampton, NJ 1978

MEMORIES

Dad's Tractor Rides, 1979

Left to Right: Bugger, Aunt Caroline, Mom

Mom's Handmade 12x12 Divorce Quilt

Good Times

Ellen &
Julie,
Hampton,
NJ,
1978-79

Mom Mom,
Pop Pop,
Julie & Me,
1978

The
Queen
Of
Cherry
Hill,
NJ,
1978

Cousins from Mom's Side

Christmas with
Shannon, Bugger & Julie

Remake of Nick, Little Tommy
and Me, 1996 & 2022

Easter, Shannon & Me,
Blue Bell, PA 1977

Jules, Me, Little Tommy and
Shannon, Mantua, NJ, 1984

Cousins from Dad's Side

Cousin Line-Ups

Reston
1980

Cow Party People
And Olan Mills

My Stage In The Finished
Basement, 1982

Rico's Visit to Reston, 1980

Tap Dancing, 1980

Soccer, 1982

Ridge Heights &
Glade Racing Suits

Me &
Audrina

Elementary School

Pioneer Day

Ethnic
Pride
Day

1985

1980

1983

LeeAnn & Dad's
Weadding

Neighborhood Play with Bahija (Director), Me (Devil), Julie (Angel) and Neighborhood Kids, 1986

Duck Beach, NC, July 27th, 1984

Hearthstone Ct, 1986. Yazoo's Situation / Choreographed Dance Routine

B-Day Parties

Camp Louise, 1989

High School

Working at People's Drugs (now CVS)

Samantha, Me & Julie

"The Great Outdoors GREATER!

Julie's Modeling Gig

Field Hockey

Chantilly Graduation at George Mason University, 1993

South Carrick
Girls
Dormitory
Spades
Night

Internship at HunterLab
and Photo Shoot at
Hazelton Labs, Reston,
VA (Monkey Ebola Stran)

Traffic Court Day

UT Concert
Choir Performance

College Begins...

UT Orientation

Penis Bandits

Craziness

Unshowered Uniform

& Fun

Amber Waves of Peyton Manning

UT Field Hockey, 95-98

Black Eye from the Last Field Hockey Tournament I'll Ever Play

Ouch...

UT Field Hockey, 95-98

Our First Gig at Great Southern Brewing Company, Now Gay Street Brewery

Yellow #5, UT, Knoxville

Reunited with Caitriona, 2019

Me & Sloane

Mercury Theater Before It Was Renovated & Converted To The Preservation Pub

Practice Space

Caitriona, Brett, Me, Rachel

400 12th Street,
Knoxville, TN

Jules and Me @ O'Charley's
on the Strip in Knoxville

Frat formal with Jocelyn,
Smith Mountain Lake, VA

Circle K, UT, Knoxville

Sloane's Party Tricks

Jesus, Mohamad and
Moses, want you
to get along!
Student Center,
UT, Knoxville, TN

UT
Graduation!
1998

Graduation
Present
to Europe,
1998

Cousin Teddy's
Rabbinic ordination

Stepbrothers

1st trip to NYC with
Andrea Büring

NYC

Schmall Onion's
Xmas Party

My Apartment

My Headshot

30th B-Day
Party

Adult
Passovers,
2009, 2010

Party!

Wedding Day

February 2nd, 2013,
Polar Dip at Lake Anne, Reston, VA

Brrrrrrrr

Small,
2013
& 2015

My Babies...

Bigger, 2017
& 2020

Pride Parade, Glamazon Booth,
2019, Washington, DC

Meeting Bob Simon, 2005 & 2015

Zoom with Dr. Farber, 202?

Cousin Reunion, 2022

PART

IV

"You want to know what's great? Last night I woke up in the middle of the night to make myself a peanut butter and jelly sandwich, and you know, it was my kitchen, it was my refrigerator, it was my apartment, and it was the best peanut butter and jelly sandwich that I have had in my entire life."

- SAINT ELMO'S FIRE

CHAPTER THIRTY-SIX

THE ROAD MOST TRAVELED

I was done with college and moved back home to Reston, a pit stop to try to figure out my next move. This time, I was at my mom's house. Mom and John, who was essentially my stepdad despite the two of them never getting married, had bought a new townhouse, so I was living with both of them. I lived there a little under a year and worked at a company with two hundred people that was basically located in our backyard. Yet I drove there and back, in a car, everyday.

I ended up getting Audrina a job there too. I prepared her for an interview with my boss by conducting mock interviews and doing role play. She received an offer. Sometimes I think our boss hired us simply to have a sounding board for her problems and to help her troubleshoot her romantic relationships, but it was great to get our feet wet in the field of human resources, the only job at the time that catered to psych majors. My favorite memory of this time was Audrina being hungover after an epic night out. I told her to take a nap under my desk while I kept watch, just like George Castanza in *Seinfeld*. We had a lot of fun, but Audrina decided to move to NYC on a dare from me. "You'll never go there," I said. I thought she was joking about wanting to go and was genuinely surprised when she called my bluff and followed through with it.

John had two sons from a prior marriage, Sebastian and Jürgen, who were born when he was stationed in Germany with the Air Force. I had met them in college a couple of times when they came to visit. But then my stepdad got a call from his ex-wife's family, asking him to make a choice: either invite them to come live with us in Reston or let them go to a German prison. They were teenagers who lacked supervision and had fallen in with a bad crowd.

When they moved in, they took the extra bedrooms upstairs because I was already the basement dweller. Upon request, they taught me the naughtiest things to say in German, including *Ich will deinen kleinen Schwanz nicht* ("I don't want your little cock"), *Du denkst, du bist schlau, aber du bist dumm* ("You think you're smart, but you're stupid"), and something to soften the blow, like *Ich liebe dich so sehr* ("I love you so much").

After a month under the same roof, John said, "This house is too crowded. I think it's time for you to move out." It didn't hurt my feelings. This time, I saw the boot coming and agreed with his assessment of the situation. I felt in control and was ready to spread my wings like the socially adept butterfly that I was, despite my brief stint with basement habitation. I knew it was time to start over again and pursue my dreams of making it in a big city, a place I swore (to myself and everyone else) that I would thrive in.

I had three choices:

1. Go to Dublin, Ireland, to live with my Irish college friend, Caitriona McCarthy, in her hometown

2. Go to Los Angeles, California, to live with Danielle, the girl I saved from sitting at the nerd table in middle school and from getting her ass kicked by the much bigger Josephine

3. Go to New York City to follow my shy but extremely brave lifelong friend, Audrina

Option three was the safest bet, and I chose it for the proximity; NYC was closest, so I could return home if things went awry. Plus, my cousin Teddy let me stay on his couch for a week while I searched for an apartment. He'd just graduated from Columbia and was going to rabbinical school on the Upper West Side of Manhattan.

Interviewing for jobs was (and is) my specialty. I had several offers rolling in. One came in at $60,000, which was an assistant to a portly man in his 60's, who required 50 hours per week in an office alone with him at 30 Rockefeller Plaza. NYU offered me $18,000 for a similar role but lacked tuition reimbursement and housing options. One of the most lucrative offers came from a company, we'll call it Schmall Onion, located next door to 30 Rock: $40,000 and unlimited commission for a sales role. This was something completely new and exciting, and the unlimited commission seemed to be the most appealing factor in my decision.

After securing a broker, I finally found my NYC apartment on the Upper East Side at the intersection of 90th Street and First Avenue. It was a 300-square-foot, junior one-bedroom, fifth-floor walk-up, which cost $1,175 per month and, according to my broker, was a steal! The landlord was planning to gut the place and renovate into a more modern apartment.

I took a little rubber ball and placed it on the floor next to the window with a fire escape. The ball quickly rolled through the living room, down the hallway, past my "junior" bedroom (only big enough for a full-sized bed and a radiator), and through the galley kitchen, then picked up speed and bounced on the wall so hard it boomeranged off the wall and back into the middle of the kitchen. I was just happy to throw parties at "my place" and use my balcony (the fire escape) to smoke with a bird's eye view of the sea of yellow taxis five stories below.

The ceiling was made of tin, painted white with intricate Victorian designs. My bathroom had black-and-white 12 x 12-inch tiles matching those of the five flights of stairs to get up to the apartment. The tiles reminded me of the music video for Tom Petty's "Don't Come Around Here No More." The toilet was surrounded by a set of steps and backed up to a wall, like a throne for a royal ass. Knowing nothing about "scald valves," I burned myself the first time I took a shower.

The building was adjacent to a check cashing place that routinely fell victim to break-in attempts, most commonly during the inconvenient hours of 1 and 4 a.m., triggering alarms that woke up the entire intersection. Another personal triumph was getting used to the street noise, which became comforting, like a lullaby of sirens and honks. Living alone liberated me from any semblance of decorum. I could bend over backward in the mirror and check out my own butthole, something I'd never seen! For the record, it's a starfish, not a cauliflower.

Once I settled in, I invited my mom for a visit. We went to the local grocery store and noticed little black boxes with flashing red lights under the shelves. "Those are rat detectors," the C-Town attendant explained. Mom came down the aisle holding some eggs and matzah to make a meal I thought she had invented and should have patented called fried matzah. Upon further research (Google), it's called Classic Matzo Brei. Anyway, we both caught sight of a dozen hot firefighters still in their protective gear, one more gorgeous than the next. I said, "Hi, how's it going?" to the best looking one, batting my eyelashes. "Did you know those are rat detectors?" I asked.

"No, gross," he said, backing away and not appreciating the public service announcement.

Mom admonished me for being crude.

"At least I didn't tell him about my gorgeous butthole!" I announced as loudly as I could.

I wonder what happened to those beautiful boys. I think of the devastating day that was 9/11 and cry for those firefighters.

CHAPTER THIRTY-SEVEN

FROSH MEAT

My office at Schmall Onion had excellent views of St. Patrick's Cathedral. Every day I had to make my way through the thick crowd packing themselves in front of *The Today Show*, hoping to get on TV. The 52-block walk to work became a sight so familiar that I'd often get a sense of déjà vu, as though' I'd seen it all in a TV show, film, or photograph.

One day, as I was descending the stairs to the subway, a horde of people rushing to get to work were ascending on the opposite side of the railing, and a man punched me in the face. No rhyme or reason, and it hurt like hell. I saw stars circling my head like I was in a Bugs Bunny cartoon. I turned to confront him, but he'd already disappeared into the crowd.

When I saw the movie *The Boiler Room*, which came out the next year, it reminded me of the culture of my company. The NYC branch was under the hegemony of my manager Ryan and his two sidekicks Jasper and George, who were three entitled, White, privileged men. The job required frequent (almost daily) work outings for dinner, happy hours, team meetings, and, worst of all, sales calls. Ryan, an overweight former lacrosse athlete with a bad cocaine habit, insisted on tagging along one day in late July to an office in Greenwich village. It was so hot that it felt like we were walking outside into a bowl of steaming soup, and none of us knew where we were going.

Down in the depths of hell (the subway station), the broiling air made Ryan sweat profusely. To distract us all from watching him melt, he ear-raped everyone on the platform with a story about his neighbor ringing him at 2 a.m. to complain about the noise from his booty call. "We shook the bed shook so hard, my pictures fell off the wall," he bragged.

"I hoped you tipped the hooker well," I replied.

I don't understand why he thought it was acceptable to discuss his sexual escapades with his subordinates. Like the "Sexual Harassment" SNL skit with Tom Brady, I guess he didn't understand the fundamentals:

- ✔ Be handsome.
- ✔ Be attractive.
- ✔ Don't be unattractive.

Underground, the air smelled of piss and garbage, like the way I imagine a vulture's mouth might smell after a meal of roadkill in Death Valley. The unpleasantness increased exponentially with the heat; temps were in the upper 90s that day.

It didn't matter how much deodorant I applied, I'd always wind up needing a shower the minute I stepped outside onto the stoop of my building, located 13 blocks from the subway and an equal 13 blocks away from work. In the winter, the freezing air shot out of the tunnel every time a train came whipping by, blowing my hair into a maelstrom of knots. There was no way to dress appropriately for the drastic temperature changes.

I think I might have been a little depressed at the time. My mind was on a constant negative loop, envisioning someone pushing me in front of a train or stabbing me to death. NYC was full of 12 million people by day and eight million at night, which somehow made me feel more alone than ever. It didn't help that at the time I was listening to the song "Blue" by Eiffel 65 on repeat and was reading James Patterson's *Cat and Mouse*, a book about a serial killer on the loose in Manhattan.

I wasn't good at keeping up with groceries, so it was a rare occasion when I brought friends over to my apartment. Joanne, who was in billing, came over once after a company happy hour, one where I clearly should have soaked up the alcohol with food. I dumped a block of frozen ground beef on the stove and kept turning it over to scrape the cooked parts off and expose the frozen layer beneath. Joanne, wary of my process, said, "Oh wow, I've never seen anyone cook meat this way."

My first day in the office, I was given the nickname "Frosh" by a self-proclaimed cool-girl clique were only a year older than me and who never told me what it meant. I can only assume the name was a dig about being fresh meat, or maybe a freshman? They also complained to management about the way our Indian coworker spoke to people over the phone; they didn't like how aggressive and loud her voice became, especially when she spoke to our third-party vendors. Moreover, I was the only Jewish employee, and these dicks made me decorate the Christmas tree by myself.

Some of the perks were nice. The company profited well from the sweat off our backs and pushed us constantly with daily stand-ups and weekly contests with dollar bills taped to the wall. The rewards included picking what music to listen to (my go-tos were Fiona Apple and Natalie Imbruglia) and being able to control the thermostat. Schmall Onion also spared no expense for training. They took us to conferences in San Francisco and a local trip to Fire Island for an all-day training retreat that included a train ride, a chartered boat, and a giant beach house for the day. We also had a group outing to the *David Letterman Show* right after his open-heart surgery.

And that Indian coworker the cool-girl clique complained about? Her name was Rashmi, and she became my first Indian friend. She taught me more than all the male managers and wannabe NYC socialites combined. I learned how to be succinct and direct, and she introduced me to Indian food and taught me how to say "water" in Urdu (*pani*). At first, the meal triggered a response of pure chaos in my stomach. I'm talking white-hot cramps and the polar opposite of the ravioli effect, but once my system processed the initial spice shock, I started to crave it. It's now my favorite hangover food, which I believe could replace the standard pre-colonoscopy prep in the field of gastrointestinal diseases.

The company challenged us to meet a certain quota by Thanksgiving, and after exceeding it we were awarded a night out on the town, complete with being picked up in a brand-new stretch Cadillac Escalade limousine and a dinner at Peter Luger's Steakhouse.

The group dinner lasted four hours longer than intended. Marylin handed me ecstasy and said, "Let's take this and go dancing!"

I'd never been to the infamous Limelight club. I later learned how notorious it was for being a "drug supermarket" where heavy drugs including ecstasy (MDMA), cocaine, and Rohypnol were used to lure patrons. We went directly to the front of the dance floor to get the best view of the drag queen dressed in a red patent leather dominatrix outfit, performing on stage. I couldn't take my eyes off her. She noticed and motioned for me to join her on stage.

All my NYC dreams came true that night! I was dancing for an audience, people were clapping, and a drag queen was including me, truly seeing me for who I was—a performer! Or it was MDMA.

CHAPTER THIRTY-EIGHT

THREE OGRES AND 32 BEERS LATER...

Sometimes I'd go out with the cool kids and exclude management, which was difficult to pull off since our bullpen office kept us in close quarters—contract recruiters on the right side and permanent staff on the left. Each side had multiple pods, each with six desks facing each other in a rectangle. My pod included Connie, the upper-crust Manhattan aristocrat; Rashmi from Long Island, the only married woman at our branch who had children; and Robby, a tall, green-eyed North Dakotan with blond curly hair who was an aspiring model and hadn't quite come out of the closet. There was also Layla from New England, a beautiful Persian who talked with her hands, wore long leather boots and tight cashmere sweaters, and was mean as a snake; and Jasper, a taller, thin, less attractive version of Robby who had floppy hair like John Glover in my favorite Christmas movie, *Scrooged*, was from Texas, and grew up with an abusive father.

Everyone knew Jasper was in love with Robby, but in reality, everyone was. He was adorable and had recently lost his mom to cancer. His sadness made him so endearing that everyone just wanted to make him feel better. Robby and I shared dreams of making it in NYC and thought, at the very least, we should try to be extras in a movie or TV show. We spent a large portion of our commission check ($300) on headshots. Robby didn't like his and wouldn't give anyone a copy. I put 30 copies of my headshot and acting resume out into the ether. For some reason, maybe my chucklesome miscellaneous section, I never got a call.

Robby introduced me to his German friend, Sonja Hofmann. Sonja and I connected immediately. Our common ground was a mutual obsession with sushi. We found an all-you-could-eat sushi joint located 40 city blocks south of my apartment. We ate as much rice as we could but then realized the fish was the best part, and the rice was filling us up like the birds who exploded and forced everyone to start throwing confetti at weddings instead. We'd hide the excessive rice in our purses, then walk (waddle) home to burn off the meal.

One night, I had an audition for a talent scout in a SoHo speakeasy. Sonja came along as my wingwoman. We arrived at the venue at 9 p.m. and kept ordering drinks until my name was finally called—at 2 a.m.! Everyone in the audience appeared to be sleeping. I sang Stevie Wonder's "Wish" and slurred my way through it, forgetting an entire verse and mixing up the words like a salad. I'm pretty sure I heard laughter from a table in the back. My performance was so embarrassing, but the band asked me to sing one more song. I chose Bonnie Raitt's "Love Me Like a Man," and Sonja said I rocked the house, waking up everyone seated around her. But we left without even giving my number to the manager, something I'd usually do in the hope of getting called back to perform. I thought I blew it. Plus, we both had to work the next day and were exhausted. Following my dreams with a day job wasn't working out.

My friendship with Sonja was beautiful. We spent all our free time together. She taught me how to make spätzle, an irregularly shaped pasta with simple ingredients: egg, flour, and water. Sonja's job was so much cooler than mine. She was a food photographer and worked for Isaac Hays (who played "Chef" on the animated sitcom *South Park*) to make his cookbook, *Cooking with Heart and Soul*. She also taught me some German and helped me understand the concept of *Kollektivschuld*, the notion of a national collective guilt for perpetuating the Holocaust and other atrocities during World War II. I always thought Germans hated me, but as it turns out, German people are nice. Only hateful people hate me for being Jewish. And they probably have a lot of hate for a lot of people, for a myriad of reasons.

At work, Robby was Jasper's favorite subject, but the night Robby turned down Jasper to instead go out with Sonja and me was a huge problem. Jasper went on a warpath to destroy me professionally. The next day, I arrived at work at 8:15 a.m. and was immediately summoned to the conference room by Ryan, Jasper, and George, all of whom were over six feet tall and towered above me like ogres. They wore expressions making it clear the situation would be ugly.

They sat closely together at a conference table meant for 20. I sat across from them. "You're late and you smell like you've been drinking," they said.

"I doubt that; my shower has no scald valves," I protested.

But Jasper must have spent his evening arranging this moment. He'd already prepared a letter, which he slid across the desk along with a pen, then pointed to the signature line and said, "You need to sign this if you want to keep your job."

The letter was a boilerplate probation document with template verbiage observing "unprofessional actions." To keep my employment, I needed to come in by 8 a.m. every day and discontinue any social interaction with the staff that included alcohol.

After that, I became like my parents and arrived no later than 7 a.m., and I often stayed after hours. Everyone took notice of my impressive numbers; some were really jealous, which was fantastic, but my main motivation was getting more commission so I could hightail it out of the city. My base salary alone was not enough to survive in Manhattan in 1999.

One Friday, I caught a glimpse of the time on my computer: 11 p.m. *What the F am I doing here?* I thought. The bubble of confidence I felt from making it in the Big Apple was quickly deflating. I was also terribly lonely, so I bought an aquarium and fish to keep me company.

A few weeks later, the "To:" line of one of Ryan's emails must have auto-generated a group email alias when he sent a dirty message about testicles, likely meant for his former lacrosse buddies, to every employee in the NYC office and his management chain. It spread all over the country at the speed of light. I didn't get a chance to read it in its entirety because he ran to my desk like a giant troll to check my inbox first, but he wasn't fast enough. He stuck his sweaty armpits in my face, scrambling my mouse around frantically until he found his note to delete. I knew it wasn't meant for me the moment I received it and had immediately sent it to my friend Marylin, with the subject "Print now," as we both despised Ryan. Marylin took the hard copy and faxed it to the corporate management team. Ryan was fired by the end of the business day.

A high school friend named Sally invited me to a music festival in West Virginia in May 2000, where we dropped acid and laughed for hours until everyone (but me) passed out spooning in a tent. The Recipe Family Cookout was my first Bluegrass festival. I stayed up to soul search by drinking 32 beers in a row while everyone slept. By the time the sun had come up over the horizon and the Capon Bridge Mountains, I had finally made the definitive decision to give up on my big NYC dreams. Everyone said I needed to stick it out a full year to become a real New Yorker. I told them if nine months was enough time to create a human, it's enough time to figure out who I really am—a suburban girl.

In the end, I made enough commission to double my base salary, but I spent almost every penny on standard NYC entertainment: bars, Broadway shows, restaurants, speakeasies, clubs, and fabulous clothes. I saved just enough for the $1,000 down payment on my Reston condo. Through my mother and her team (my sister and childhood Reston friend Alexis) I purchased a condo sight unseen. Mom sacrificed her commission to pay the closing costs and knew it was kismet when she found a bat, a creature known for its nocturnal habits, peacefully taking a nap while hanging from the gutter over the back patio. I worked with my manager's manager, Kent Perry, in Boston to get an interview and subsequent transfer to the closest office to Reston available—in McLean, Virginia. Twenty years later I got Kent a job with my company. Karma *is* a God, Taylor Swift!

Audrina, Robby, and Sonja, along with my high school friends Randa and Kate and a bunch of coworkers, all bid me farewell from NYC the same way we spent most nights, getting shitfaced. Sonja was happy to finally speak German with Jürgen and John. The next day, after making about a million trips up and down my fifth-floor walk-up stairs for the move, Jürgen was so hungover that he puked on the side of Mom's purple Mercury Capri at a rest stop on the way home. I gave him my fish in a bag and asked him to blow into a straw periodically so the fish could breathe and he could focus on something other than his nausea.

I was proud of myself for having the audacity to believe I belonged in the city and the self-preservation to know when to move on. New York taught me how to win and how to fail with grace. The failures stung, but they helped me see that I could do more difficult things. I gave it my best shot, and I'm proud of having the courage to chase my *Sex and the City* dreams. Failure gave me the confidence to know when to leave, which was the best decision for me. I was thrown into the fire in my very first real job out of college. It was a male-dominated, misogynistic environment. I took some hits, but I still thrived.

CHAPTER THIRTY-NINE

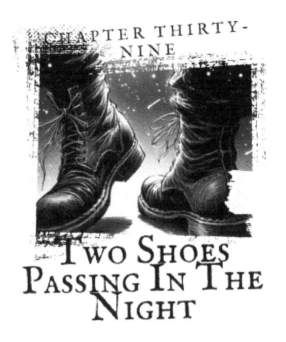

Two Shoes Passing In The Night

When I was at UT, right before my toxic relationship with Jason ended, I met Ricky. Ricky was best friends with Sloane's boyfriend (now husband), Bart. We met at a party at Sloane's apartment in Neyland Hills. Both boys were from a town outside Chattanooga. Someone brought a tank of nitrous oxide, and everyone tried it because they wanted to know what the shortest and best-recorded high ever felt like. Apparently, it was the closest thing to heroin, one drug I never had the guts or desire to try. (For the record, it was the same with meth, crack, and PCP, although in my twenties I might have accidentally smoked weed laced with PCP at a rowhome party in Baltimore with Lainey. Not sure if it was that or the Everclear ice luge shots that made me want to rock myself to death on the bathroom floor?) Anyhoo, Ricky was a handsome, fit, green-eyed dazzler who made me wish I hadn't invited Jason. It's possible I made my feelings observable, but the seduction was very low key.

A few days later, I passed Ricky as I was leaving work at the UT library. I was wearing khaki cut-off shorts, a misshapen, oversized mustard-colored golf shirt, and my unwashed hair in a side braid, a trick I used to avoid showering. Our eyes locked. I smiled and said, "Hey Ricky." He replied with, "Hey, beautiful." My whole body blushed. I called Sloane and suggested we should do a double date sometime.

The boys took us to a Mexican restaurant where we drank way too much tequila. Bart borrowed some dude's guitar from the mariachi band, and they both serenaded us with Marty Robbins's "El Paso," an eight-verse song plus an outro about falling in love with a brown-eyed girl only to die in her arms after being shot in the heart. Ricky kept his eyes on me the entire time. I realized then that I was the one getting seduced.

We went back to their apartment in Neyland Hills and played strip poker, but Ricky was the only unlucky one forced to remove his clothes. Sloane giggled and teased him about his protruding nipples, similar to the "big ears" ridicule I got when Sloane and I first met. When it was time for me to go back to my shack on 12th street, Ricky walked me out to my car. Once we hit the parking lot, as if on cue, snowflakes started falling onto our hair and faces. Snow was so rare in Knoxville; it made the moment seem straight out of a fairytale. The light streamed and flickered from the streetlamps above when Ricky pulled me to him, touched my face, and gently kissed me. I was hooked.

Ricky and I had an on-and-off relationship for eight years. Mom and John gifted us both a trip to Europe as my graduation present. We traveled to Germany first and rented a black Mercedez that took us all over the country. Part of the trip was in Düsseldorf, where John had been staying for work. He introduced us to the happy hour crowd at the bar in the basement of his apartment building and the bartender, Andrea Büring. Andrea was my age and took us out on the town. Six months later, she came to visit me in Reston. She reinforced the concept that German people are nice and deeply ashamed of their former association with Nazis.

Ricky and I went to Amsterdam, but he refused to smoke pot, even where it was legal, leaving me to smoke alone in a darkly lit coffee house, right before getting onto a glass-topped canal boat that glided all over the city. I bought something comparable to strawberry Yoohoo to drink on the boat. The weather was overcast, but it was a very hot August day. Like the movie *Anchorman*, after my first sip I realized "milk was a bad choice." We also went to Paris to see the Louvre and then met back up with Mom and John in Prague, where we slept on uncomfortable beds and watched the news that included a topless meteorologist. Prague remains the second most beautiful city I've been to, after Reston.

We went to a wedding for one of Ricky's high school friends, where the bride had written a poem for her husband-to-be and read it aloud during the ceremony: "I love Jesus Christ, who bled to death on a cross for me. I love Jesus Christ, who sent me my love, Corey. I love Corey, because he also loves Jesus Christ."

Later that day, I asked Ricky if it bothered him that I wasn't Christian.

He said, "No, because we have so many other things in common."

"Good," I said, "because if we ever got married, Jesus would not be mentioned in song, sermon, or poem form."

I ignored the clouds of resentment accumulating as I created a picture of our Jesus-less future. Those words would have a lasting impact on our relationship.

In the end, Ricky wanted a drug-free, Christian wife who he was sure to meet in the afterlife. According to him—and almost every other devout Christian I know—blind faith in Jesus Christ was the only way to be admitted into heaven. So I used the only card I had: I told him he would have a hard time finding someone who loved him as much as I did. And I meant it. I thought he was *the* one, but the chemistry, fun, and my intense love for him weren't enough.

The night before Sloane and Bart's wedding, Ricky brought me over to his apartment, across the courtyard from Sloane's. We sat on the couch, facing each other, and he asked, "What happens when our kids ask if you believe in God?" He was crying.

"I don't have that figured out just yet, but I think the truth might be best," I said. It felt like the nail in the coffin of our relationship, for the moment.

Sloane chose me as her "maid of dishonor," which was the lesser of two evils because it eliminated the need to decide between her two sisters. But for me, it was really hard to keep my attitude light, to hide the incredible shame I felt for envying Sloane, instead of feeling happy for them both. Ricky was one of Bart's groomsmen. I tried my best to put on a happy face, keeping the heartache of our most recent breakup to myself. I held Sloane's dress and smiled in all the pictures, especially the one with just me and Ricky's kind parents. I heard they kept it on their fridge well after we'd broken up, which was a nice consolation prize. Sloane and Bart's wedding was booze-free and located in a church basement. Sloane's dress and flowers were nice though.

The penultimate "last time" I saw Ricky was after I'd moved home to Reston and worked for a large defense contractor. I had single-handedly orchestrated a UT college recruiting trip just to see him again. He'd been working on a plan B, to pursue an MBA, since his dream of becoming a pilot never panned out. Two additional male coworkers accompanied me: an older gentleman whose name and face I can't remember, and a cute Irish guy a few years younger than me named Paxton. Ricky came by the recruiting fair and said he couldn't meet me until much later, but he promised to come by my hotel room after he was finished. I was devastated and proceeded to go out and get as drunk as possible.

Before returning to the hotel, I finished a bottle of wine. Once there, Paxton joined me in my room for what was meant to be a final drink but turned out to be a transformative moment. In a pleasantly surprising turn of events, he revealed his feelings for me, completely shifting the dynamic between us. His heartfelt declaration came unexpectedly from this charming and attractive young man, altering the course of our relationship dramatically.

Ricky wasn't dropping by because he loved me and couldn't live without me, as I'd hoped. He just wanted a booty call. I completely forgot about that when Paxton kissed me, the same moment Ricky dinged my cell to inform me he was on his way! I shot up and said, "You've got to go, Paxton!" and shooed him out so quickly he didn't have time to put his shoes back on. He carried them in his hands down the hall, passing Ricky on the way back to his room.

Ricky told me he was coming down with a cold and just wanted to snuggle, which advanced quickly into the topic of condoms. However, Ricky had been involved in several relationships since we'd last seen each other, so when he continued to undress after admitting he didn't have one, I stopped him. "When was the last time you had unprotected sex?" I asked.

"'It's been a while," he said. But for him that could have meant last month, last week, or even yesterday. I became furious.

"I'm sorry," I said, "I just don't trust you anymore!" Then I kicked him out. Or maybe he left. I can't remember because I was so very drunk.

I realize the irony in my actions, as I had just condemned infidelity only to find myself with two different men in my bed within a short span of 30 minutes. However, my intentions were not merely about physical gratification. I longed for Ricky to express an unwavering commitment to me. I didn't want a booty call. I wanted Ricky to tell me he couldn't live without me and throw his bible out the window, to propose marriage and realize I would love him in this life and possibly the next if there was such a thing. But he didn't.

The next day, my regret-propelled hangover convinced me I needed another shot at a last encounter. Ricky took me to Applebee's, a restaurant I refuse to set foot in to this day, and then to the airport. Sitting on sticky pleather seats across from Ricky and a classic combo appetizer I couldn't bear to eat, I realized my love would never be requited. However, the attraction was still there. At the airport we joked about finding a bathroom or a broom closet to say goodbye properly in, but I knew I'd just end up in the same place I was the night before. Instead, we said goodbye at the base of an escalator. He was about to ascend, and I was going the opposite direction, headed toward my flight. We embraced, and I said something I'd heard before but couldn't recall where: "It was better to have loved and lost than to have never loved at all." He said nothing, but he held eye contact with me all the way up the escalator. Pleased with my display of integrity, maturity, and grace, I boarded the plane and cried on Paxton's shoulder the whole way home.

The next and final time I saw Ricky was when I was visiting UT for a football game. Lainey and I tried to go back every third weekend in October to see the Alabama game. On game day, I spotted him from the passenger seat of Lainey's car, walking into a liquor store on the strip in Knoxville. It took every ounce of dignity to restrain myself from jumping out of the car while we were stopped at a light. I had 30 seconds to decide whether I should chase him and try one last time to make him love me, but I froze. I was consumed with fear of the inevitable rejection, and I knew I couldn't take another heartbreak from this man. The light turned green, and Ricky disappeared inside the store. Lainey looked at me sympathetically and drove on. "I just couldn't subject myself to another round of humiliation," I said. Also, there was a little voice in my head telling me I would someday find a man who would accept me just the way I was and love me the way I deserved, with zero conditions.

Going through my archive of VHS tapes, I found one that high-lighted a three-day road trip from Ricky's apartment in Houston to San Antonio and back again. A thinner version of myself with a surprisingly Southern accent flooded the screen and speakers. It made my skin crawl. As my kids would say, "It was so cringe." I don't like hearing my speaking voice on tape because in my head I sound louder and more commanding. On tape playing back to me, it sounds nasal and wimpy. Was I trying to sound more like Ricky, with his accent? I was a version of myself that worked at the time, but that time had passed. I grew out of Ricky and grew into me.

PART

V

"You know, when I was nineteen, Grandpa took me on a roller coaster. Up, down, up, down. Oh, what a ride. I always wanted to go again. You know, it was just interesting to me that a ride could make me so frightened, so scared, so sick, so excited and so thrilled all together. Some didn't like it. They went on the merry-go-round. That just goes around. Nothing. I like the roller coaster. You get more out of it."

- PARENTHOOD

CHAPTER FORTY

A MAGICAL PRINCE

Turning 30 was truly the end of an era. At work, everyone my age, and 80 percent of those younger, were already married with kids. The defense contracting, conservative world imposed endless interrogations as to what was taking me so long to settle down.

On my 30th birthday, the younger, unwed coworkers showered me with gifts, hung a sign that read, "Behind every successful woman is . . . herself," gave me thoughtfully written cards, and decorated my office ostentatiously. All the married folks thought it was weird. Yet every other week there was an engagement party, bridal shower, or baby shower for my coworkers. Like hot cross buns, I, along with another unmarried female colleague, was expected to contribute anywhere from $5 to $50 and plan them. Eventually I complained to my boss who said, "It's not a punishment because you're single; it's because you're so good at organizing fun events!"

My sister baked the most beautiful cupcakes in the shape of dolls to share with everyone at work. The next day she threw me the most epic party at North Hill Park in Reston, complete with Beer

Olympics, a chartered party bus bound for DC afterward, and my closest friends and family. Even Little Tommy showed up. He was the first cousin to visit and begin to mend fences from the family breakup. His parents, my Uncle Tommy and Aunt Eileen, affectionately dubbed him "Little Tommy," despite his and his younger brother Nick's imposing stature, and it's a bit of a family joke. Little Tommy clinched the national wrestling championship in high school and subsequently pursued a career as a state trooper, while Nick has proven himself a formidable force in powerlifting, securing victories in no less than six World's Strongest Man competitions.

Julie wore a shirt that read, "You can have my sister." I could be a pain in the ass, and my teenage years certainly didn't help our adolescent relationship, but there has never been a bigger champion for me than Julie. She's the most loving and caring sister anyone could ask for. Throughout our lives, anytime something terrible happened to us, even when we lived in separate states, Julie telepathically knew it. Similar to Will from the TV series *Stranger Things* detecting the presence of the Mind Flayer, she experienced the hairs on the back of her neck standing on end and sensed a foreboding sensation the evening I had my car accident during high school, just moments before I chugged my milk. That same eerie premonition struck her the morning I underwent the procedure for eight stitches around my left eye following the field hockey mishap.

I left the defense contracting company for a much smaller one that offered more money and responsibility. On my first day, my new boss, Kathleen, paraded me around the office, introducing me to each person individually. A man named Dan had his own office at the end of the hall, opposite mine. Kathleen said, "Dan, this is Ellen, our new HR manager. Ellen, tell Dan about yourself."

"Hi, I'm Ellen, the new HR manager," I said like a vapid moron. Dan laughed and said, "I'm Dan, the old software engineer."

Several months later, another coworker told me that Dan had a crush on me, but I didn't believe him. Dan has the most piercing blue eyes, the kind that make you feel like he's seeing right through you and into your soul. The icy electric pattern of starburst furrows in his irises make Bono's seem dull in comparison. I didn't take the coworker's admission seriously because Dan was not only the most attractive man I'd ever seen—so fine all the lunch ladies from the office cafeteria nicknamed him "Handsome Dan"—but was six years my junior, Hollywood fit, and absolutely adorable. Way out of my league.

In February 2009, I went skiing with about 20 friends at Deep Creek's Wisp Resort. While I was there, Dan sent me a Facebook friend request on Valentine's Day. I informed my housemates, five couples and 10 single people, that I still had it, giving us another reason to celebrate with a gravity bong before hitting the slopes. I showed Lainey a shirtless picture he'd sent me, and she showed it to Cameron, her now-husband, telling him, "I think you should start working out."

Dan and I started dating immediately upon my return home. Our first date was a day trip to Liberty Ski Resort, one of three ski resorts located an hour from Reston. It was Dan's first time skiing, and he took to it immediately. I envisioned a future of family ski trips, maybe even one out west or the Alps, which I still have yet to ski. It took years for him to tell me he really didn't like skiing. But he had done it for me. This guy was a keeper.

I was wary of jumping in too quickly with a colleague, especially given my poor track record of dating Shane, the marketing director at my old job, which had inevitably forced me to simultaneously quit my job and kick him out of my condo. Shane was funny and charming, and everyone loved him—unless he was wasted. What ultimately led to our demise was when he threw a cake at me during the company party I'd spent weeks organizing, ruining my only formal jacket, which had a big, black fur hood. Shane turned out to be a raging alcoholic, and I was understandably reluctant to make the same mistake when I started dating Dan.

I decided on the arbitrary number of 17 dates with Dan before making our relationship official. Most of our coworkers and management chain didn't know we were dating until they got an invite to our wedding. Those childhood acting classes from the Reston Community Center came in super handy.

I was planning for the most epic Passover on record, a 50-person Seder! I must have been experiencing a stroke of clairvoyance, because during the planning I had the foresight to reserve a spot on the guest list for an aptly named "TBD/Magical Prince"—Dan. Over time, Dan proved himself a good fit for the role. This was the second year my dad, LeeAnn, and Brandon attended our new version of Passover, a giant step in the right direction for all four of my parents, who hadn't been under one roof since our college graduations.

Dad gave an unexpectedly emotional speech about how proud he was of his all grown-up, successful daughters. The most heartwarming part was his adept insight into what I'd been trying to do. He publicly acknowledged the experience of Passover as a gift that was more special than any material goods because it brought people of different backgrounds together. It was the first time I felt like he truly saw my intentions and didn't underestimate me. He said, "This is the purpose of Passover, sharing the story of our past so we aren't doomed to repeat it." I wanted to recreate that feeling of belonging by including non-Jews in my culture. It's the best way to encourage positive association and reinforcement with Jewish people and to create lasting memories with our forever friends, like the Bernadottes.

When Lainey and I made a list of the qualities we wanted from an ideal mate after reading *He's Just Not That Into You,* it proved to be very beneficial in finding a husband. With each failed relationship, I learned more about what I needed and who I wanted to marry. I didn't just wake up one day and say, "I deserve better"; I had to step inside the shadow world, go through each agonizing first date, and endure each painful relationship until its doomed end. I had to bury them deep enough underground that they couldn't resurrect.

Every failure taught me something about myself and what I could and could not tolerate. I learned that I'm not responsible for curing alcoholism or depression, nor for turning someone's life around when their childhood dreams didn't come to fruition. Cheating and physical abuse are not okay, ever. My happiness was never going to be contingent upon the behavior of someone else.

CHAPTER FORTY-ONE

PLATE TECTONICS

I woke up alone in my condo at 5:14 a.m. on July 16, 2010, to the sound of my cat, Sven, jumping off the top of my curio cabinet onto the hardwood floor with a loud thud. However, as I became more conscious, I realized that Sven had died two years prior and that the noise was actually a 3.6-magnitude earthquake that shook from West Virginia to Connecticut. Dan and I had been dating steadily for six months, and he'd already asked me to pick out a ring. I was anxious for him to give it to me and refused to move in with him until he proposed. I'd be turning 35 in less than two weeks and was feeling the biological pressure to procreate, ASAP.

That evening, en route to pick up dinner, he suggested the salad bar at our local grocery store, and I lost my ever-loving mind. "Giant salad bar again? It's Friday night! I know you like saving money, but this is ridiculous! Also, why did you even ask me to pick out a ring if you weren't going to propose? I'm about to be middle-aged!" I cried, stomping my feet like a toddler having a meltdown.

"Calm down, Hellman, I'm planning something special. Don't ruin the surprise," he said with a controlled self-possession I'd eventually need to investigate.

We picked up our $7 salads and headed back home to watch my new favorite female comedian, Lisa Lampanelli. I'd just seen her a month prior in person with my friends on a bus trip to NYC. The bus caught fire on the way there and got lost on the way back, which prolonged the 10-hour trip an additional six hours. I was sitting on the brown suede sectional couch that I resented for its individual seats with cup holders in the arm rests that prevented me from snuggling with Dan.

I laughed at an insult Lampanelli's comedy was known for, and Dan clicked pause on the remote. I started to protest, thinking, *Maybe the joke was too racy for him?* But then I saw the black velvet box in his hands. Inside was a diamond ring in the shape of a flower. It shimmered like a million jittery lighting bugs were trapped within it. As he knelt down on one knee, I think he said, "I love you, Ellen. Will you marry me?" but I had lost the ability to hear anything but the rush of blood from my galloping heartbeat and was merely lip-reading at that point. He had tricked me into thinking this would be a normal night when we'd eat our boring salads while sitting on the jail couch that forced us to compartmentalize our affections until the TV portion of the evening was over. Instead, we went to Mom's for surprise number two!

At Mom and John's midtown condo, all my friends and siblings had been summoned. The champagne was already flowing before we arrived, since we had run late due to my temper tantrum and Dan's subsequent diversion. Others may remember that date because of the earthquake, but I'd like to believe that the earth moved that morning in preparation for our impending engagement. The tectonic plates were celebrating before I even knew! It took 12 more years before I let Dan throw out that ugly sectional brown couch.

With the exception of my high school graduation, because I was living with Dad and LeeAnn at the time, my mom and Julie initiated and organized every detail of my milestone celebrations. For my wedding, Mom and Julie conducted planning sessions where I got to choose the colors and themes for my engagement party, shower, and wedding. We went to nine wedding dress shops and found the perfect one, which we ordered online for a quarter of the price.

Julie persuaded me to "make at least one thing about the groom" and convinced me to have the wedding at Virginia Tech, where she, Dan, and more than half the wedding party had graduated. I color-coded the wedding party: pale yellow for old childhood friends Audrina, Sally, and Samantha; Tennessee Orange for college friends Jocelyn, Lainey, and Kim; and red for Virginia Tech grads Julie, Mina, and Heather. Julie was my maid of honor, of course. In total, the wedding cost $22,000, split between my parents. I cut corners, but Mom would not let me budge on seat covers. She chose Tennessee Orange, the color signifying our journey back to each other, and she wanted the room to look and feel majestic.

A few years prior, Sloane and I had traveled to London, Stonehenge, and Edinburgh together, and we would visit each other every year, sometimes twice. Before I got engaged, she insisted she should be the officiant, given how much we'd been through, how much she knew me and my family, and her flair for the dramatic. I knew she would kill it. But a week before the wedding, she sent me an email saying she couldn't come because of an Easter pageant for her daughter. This slap in particular felt like I'd been stung by a murder hornet. I'd specifically chosen Easter for my wedding to bring down the headcount, figuring those who truly loved me would choose me over Jesus. So this was a shocking blow, as my plan had backfired in more ways than one.

Passover is always linked within a week to Easter, and I have four Rabbi cousins, none of whom were able to attend. Sloane and I were agnostic; every chance we could get we made fun of Ricky for being a devout Christian. Bart was a staunch atheist, and our conversations often led to the creation of a new religion. However, we kept getting stuck on death and disability and decided against the rollout.

Sloane's Easter-related excuse was clearly a cover. I couldn't imagine Easter being more important than my wedding in Sloane's world. So I never responded to the email, and I deleted her number from my phone, her address from my computer, and every trace of her from my life, completely.

The most difficult part of my coming-of-age story was the wait. It took so long! The uncertainty of not knowing anything about my future, like who or if I was ever going to marry, was painful. I'd kept thinking things like, *Will anyone ever really love me? Will I ever have kids? Are these my real friends? Is this the right career? Is this the best location for me? What is the best medication to combat hormonal acne?* Wait! That last one I have an answer to. It's called Accutane. And I had to sign a zillion papers promising to use two forms of birth control so that I didn't give birth to a fire monster. But I had waited so long for this, and Sloane wouldn't be there.

My cousins, Brad and Mark, had been on standby for the wedding as my officiants, just in case Sloane flaked, as I had the feeling she might. My favorite wedding picture has neither me nor my husband in it; it's of Audrina smiling genuinely at Brad, who she caught at a teary moment. When I asked him about it, he said, "When you came through the doors you just looked so happy and beautiful, it made me remember you as a little girl. I kept flashing back and forth from the image of the beautiful grown-up woman in front of me to the child I see whenever I look at you, because I've known you your whole life. It really got me good."

In the end, my cousins should have been my first choice because it turned out to be the best idea in the world. The ceremony they ran as fake ordained rabbis, or as I like to say, "getting my cousins to marry me," still gives me uncontrollable giggles because at heart I'm a 12-year-old. They were funny, entertaining, brilliant, and at ease in front of over a hundred people, including my close friends and family. But the biggest highlight was having two family members there who truly love and accept me for who I am—an authentic fuck-up who took way too long to become the successful, contributing-to-society adult I am today.

I look back on the time when I felt like I'd always be a bridesmaid, never a bride, watching so many of my friends get married and have kids before I even had a real prospect of a marriage suitor. I wish I could just go back and tell myself, "It's going to work out!" I sought the type of career to enable financial independence because I wanted to "have it all," like Liz Lemon from *30 Rock*. Balancing my career aspirations while collecting irons for my reproductive fire seemed impossible, but I knew how unfair it would be to enter into a relationship with nothing more to offer than a fading pretty face. The proposal that had eluded me in my reproductive system's prime had finally come. Thank goodness for science.

CHAPTER FORTY-TWO

PUMPING PROBLEMS

Pregnancy after age 35 is referred to as "advanced maternal age" or, another fun delineation, "geriatric pregnancy." My husband and I tried getting pregnant for two years unsuccessfully, and I worried my abortion in college was to blame. Getting pregnant required seven humiliating months of fertility treatments at Shady Grove. I'll never forget sitting in those waiting rooms. Everyone looked just as miserable as the people I'd seen in the abortion clinic waiting room all those years ago. No one said a word or even looked at each other. Acknowledgment encouraged a comparison of backstories, and I didn't want to foster false hope or discouragement. No one did. We all wanted to just get through the demeaning task of needing medical help to do what women have been capable of doing alone since the beginning of time.

I went off birth control, or as my friend Lainey says, "removed the goalie," at age 36 in 2011. At the time, I was following in my mother's footsteps, working a second job as a Zumba instructor at the women's gym in Reston. I figured if I couldn't bear children, at least

I could be in amazing shape. I'd discovered Zumba at another gym, where I'd been taking several other classes. One day, I peered into the studio and saw 50 women dancing so enthusiastically it looked more like a scene from a club in DC than an exercise room. All the ladies were hollering right along with the instructor. I slipped in the back, mid-class, then gradually made my way to the front. I never left the class, because, as you know, my favorite pastime is watching myself in front of a mirror.

Unfortunately, all the practicing in the world couldn't have helped me look skilled in the art of Latin dancing. I've got rhythm, but my broken butt, thanks to Marc Glass, is still attached to my spine. My technique (if you can call it that) is not at all like other Zumba instructors. They make it look super easy and sexy no matter what size, shape, or nationality. They make us believe that we, too, will have sex again someday this century. I can't get halfway through one song without turning into a one-eyed, one-horned, flying purple people-eater, covered in white hives and with sweat pouring out of my eyeballs and butt crack. My only saving grace was to make good music choices (mostly reggaeton) and to rip off routines from YouTube, which ultimately gave me a nice-sized group of regulars. I was proud to be part of something that gave other women confidence. I didn't know when or if I'd ever be able to have children, but teaching Zumba made me feel like I was part of something bigger, something that showcased my womanly-ness and my purpose.

One of my regular students, Gail, brought her six-year-old daughter, Julianna, to several of my classes. Julianna didn't participate in the class, but I caught her dancing in the mirror a few times. Both stayed late one day to invite me to do a Polar Dip at Lake Anne for a charity called Camp Sunshine. The charity raises funds to provide tuition for children battling life-threatening illnesses and their families. I agreed because it was for a wonderful cause, and I figured it would either jump-start my reproductive system or kill me instantly via heart attack. Spoiler alert: I didn't die, and the second round of intrauterine insemination worked!

Almost everyone had a horror story about what could go wrong during labor and birth; I was beyond nervous. I read all kinds of books to prepare me for motherhood, and I was a basket case of worry about things like listeria, preeclampsia, stillbirth, and everything else that could possibly go wrong with development in utero. It didn't help matters that I worked next to a man whose wife's due date had passed and told me about a procedure called "stripping the cervix" to get everything moving along. He made it seem perfectly natural and didn't mention anything about pain, which I'm not even sure she'd felt, but I heeded my obstetrician's recommendation and agreed to go through it. I jumped backward off the examination table, screaming so loudly my obstetrician left the room to assure my neighbors I wasn't dying. Also, it didn't work; I never went into labor naturally.

Thanks to modern medicine, being late meant I got to schedule my daughter's birthdate. I chose one that was easily translatable to a mnemonic. I became a mother on December 23, 2013, making it the happiest Christmas season of my lifetime. It took only a shot of Pitocin to induce labor, and I had a perfectly timed epidural due to lying about feeling pain before I ever really felt a contraction, because, why not? I don't understand the point of going through pain when you don't have to. In her book *I'll Show Myself Out,* Jesse Klien has a whole chapter called "Get the Epidural" where she talks about how no one expects a man to get a root canal naturally. Amen, sister!

The delivery took only eight pain- and event-free pushes! The doctor said, "You seem more excited about the fact you didn't shit yourself during birth than having an actual baby," which was hilarious, but she was wrong.

Looking into my daughter's beautiful eyes, the same shade as her fathers, I knew she recognized me as her mother, the person who'd been carrying her around, singing to her, playing music through belly-phones, swimming in warm pools every morning, and making wishes about her future and perfect health. I felt like I already understood her personality, which is kind and loving. It was magical. I did even better with my youngest—three pushes total. That has to be a world record of some kind, but an Olympic gold medal or a letter from the president should suffice.

I always assumed Dan would find watching the birth of our child extraordinary, but he was grossed out by all the blood. When the doctor asked him whether he wanted to cut the cord, he said, "Not really," but then he did it anyway, knowing I'd never let it go. Some people are so paranoid. It wasn't until he held our baby in his arms that he removed the look of aversion from his face and smiled.

The day after Audrey was born, I woke up to a visit from my in-laws. They brought us vanilla skinny lattes and chocolate croissants from Starbucks, my favorite. I got up to pee and realized the painkillers had worn off and my vagina had gained 359 pounds. I felt it ripping away from my nether region with each step, acutely aware of the stitches connecting my anus, birth canal, and rebroken tailbone. According to my obstetrician, anyone who has previously broken their tailbone to the point where it had to refuse is guaranteed to break it again during vaginal childbirth. Damn you, Marc Glass!

I gingerly walked across the room, whimpering, and no one cared. They were all too engrossed with my beautiful, healthy baby. I felt sorry for myself because I knew from that day forward I was just a vessel to make other smaller humans, and my most important job was to keep them alive. I learned all about postpartum sandwich panties, a combination of a cold pack (for swelling), a giant pad resembling a diaper, and disposable underwear. I mastered individual showers for my undercarriage, using a spray bottle every time I relieved myself, as instructed, and I took sitz baths any time I got a free minute, which was very rare. Why don't baby manuals cover this?

My sister spent the week sitting on our brown recliner every night. She placed Audrey's body between her propped-up knees so she could admire the wonder of Audrey's beauty while she slept soundly. New babies are very tired, and I cried like one the day Julie had to go back to work, which was a week later. Dad and LeeAnn came for a few days to help around the house. They taught me how to wash baby bottles correctly; everything looked sparkling and brand-new. They also helped me with food and laundry because I was a half-brained zombie, aimlessly sleepwalking from room to room and incapable of completing simple tasks, including taking showers or straightening up. Mom came over on the weekends, and my Father-in-law, Jeff, stayed with us every Wednesday for years to help us out. It really does take a village.

I was pretty good about keeping Audrey happy; she was a fantastic baby. But one day I couldn't get her comfortable. I ran through the list: hunger, sleep, change, gas, and temperature, but even my go-to warm bath didn't soothe her. I called the doctor, who suggested I put Tylenol in a bottle, but I didn't have any in the house, which I hadn't left in two months except to take Audrey to the doctor because I was insane about germs and public exposure. So, I parked outside CVS, with Audrey howling in the backseat and the windows down. Too terrified to bring her into the store, I begged each person walking by to buy Tylenol for me, offering $20 in hand. The first woman ignored me, the second man didn't speak English, and the third woman took my money and came back with Tylenol and some change. Thank you, sweet stranger.

If I could go back and talk to my former self, I would encourage her to take walks outdoors every day. When I finally took Audrey outside in March, she loved it so much that she tried to lick the wind.

———— ∞∞∞ ————

Other than breastfeeding and pumping, I felt like I'd squandered the entire five months of my (mostly unpaid) maternity leave. I felt this burden on my chest that wouldn't let up unless I made myself cry. The people who didn't have kids would say, "This is what you signed up for." All the moms would say, "Welcome to the club. This is motherhood."

I cried to my mom, who took me, Audrey, and Dan to Atlantic City the week before I had to go back to work. During the trip, I relaxed. Babies are great travelers; they just need a lot of equipment.

Looking back, I realize all my crying was probably untreated postpartum depression, and that trip was when my hormones were finally leveling out. However, I dreaded going back to work and leaving my baby in daycare. Corporate America stinks.

I was anxious about returning to the office. In 2014, breastfeeding laws were still in their infancy, and I wasn't sure where I'd be able to go to pump. I shared an office with my staff and went to discuss the matter with my manager in his office. He said nonchalantly, "It won't be a problem. You can do it in here."

I was immediately uncomfortable. "Oh, no," I said, "I don't want to put you out."

"Well, where would you like to do it?" he asked, forgetting that the company was obligated to provide a space other than a bathroom—part of a new law.

Luckily I had a friend in the contracts department named Cecilia who had her own office and invited me to come in and shut the door.

I printed a note that read, "Do not disturb, pumping in progress" and taped it to the front of the door.

Cecilia's boss was the corporate controller, a meek man in his late fifties with the temperament of a church mouse, and he looked like one too. But on that day, at that moment, he had to have his report! With no way to lock the door, he opened it before Cecilia could come around her desk to stop him. I sat facing him, trying to shield the view of my nipples stretching like udders inside the honking, transparent siphoning cups and corresponding Regina George bandeau bra. I was mortified, but I should have been angry.

On the drive home, my boobs hurt from being so engorged. The traffic was terrible and I couldn't wait to get home. I got out my Medela pumping machine, hooked it to my cow tits, and pressed the button. The cars started moving and I felt fantastic. I had won! I could work a full day and pump in the car, multitasking to save time and save me from the humiliation of being naked in front of a gross male coworker. But then life handed me another curve ball. The car in front of me made a sudden stop, I followed suit, and the warm, fresh breast milk spilled all over my dress pants. It not only ruined my Liz Lemon dreams but my only dress pants with elastic strong enough to hide my giant, unshrinking, post-baby belly, despite my wearing a postpartum girdle until I passed out from lack of oxygen.

Audrey was such a tiny, helpless, delicate creature. Picking her up and undressing her was both beautiful and scary. A few days after she was born, we got hit by a blizzard. She always looked so cold and fragile that I wanted her skin covered from head to toe at all times. Dan had read all the baby books too, and he reminded me of the skin-to-skin method. He stripped her down and tickled her pink wrinkly skin all over, and she smiled for the very first time. I secretly hated him at that moment.

———⌘———

I went back to Shady Grove while on maternity leave because I did *not* want Audrey to be an only child. Neither did Dan, who grew up as an only child. My chances of being successful at another round of insemination, especially at the age of 38, had dropped significantly, and my new doctor (my original Shady Grove doctor died in a jet-skiing accident) recommended in vitro immediately. I had to pump myself with hormones to beef up my egg count. Sometimes it required shots in the stomach, which Dan administered, except for that one time I flinched and he accidentally shot himself in the hand instead. "I've been shot!" he shouted. "Oh no! I hope your boobs don't grow bigger than mine!" I replied. And right before the surgical procedure to remove the egg, I got a big shot in the butt.

Most women going through IVF produce 10 to 20 eggs. I produced three. But all you need is one, and that one was to become my youngest daughter, Adeline! I was surprised how much the procedure to remove the eggs hurt. My tall, gorgeous, blonde, blue-eyed friend Eliza, who used to sell her eggs for thousands of dollars when we were in our twenties, never mentioned it. Maybe I just feel more pain than most women in general?

After the egg and sperm became an embryo outside of my body, they had to transfer it back into my uterus using a sonogram. On the monitor, the lining of my uterus looked like a field of tall grass. The doctor made softball analogies while we watched him "pitch" the embryo into the middle of the screen, and it rolled right along the grass, specifically where he wanted it to go. "Home run!" we cheered, feeling hopeful and nervous.

My parents seemed to take turns being there for the birth of my children. Dad and LeeAnn hadn't been there the day Audrey was born, but I got a call the next day with tearful apologies. The day of Adeline's delivery, Mom and Julie went to my friend Samantha's wedding since Julie had become a bridesmaid replacement for me, but my in-laws stayed at our house a couple of nights so I could take full advantage of the three hospital days my insurance allowed.

I was definitely the mom in the Luvs Diapers commercial who made everyone bathe in hand sanitizer before holding her firstborn. The scene switches over to when she's got two kids and pushes the younger baby into the greasy arms of an auto mechanic so she can fish something out of her purse. Adeline didn't seem to mind the slight, but she developed acid reflux and colic, which meant she needed to be held at all times. Dan found the best way to keep her comfortable was to have her straddle his knee and tap his heel to each Mississippi second. We named it the "slow tap."

I was a real nervous Nelly about SIDS and woke up multiple times a night to check both my daughters' breathing. They'd be fast asleep in their cribs, and I'd auditorily hallucinate, hearing nonexistent baby cries from the cosmos. Every time I checked, I found them back underneath their burp cloths, which only perpetuated my oxygen intake worries. I'd remove the cloth from their nose and mouth, go back to bed, then put a blanket over my face to see how long it would take to suffocate. Good riddance to those fretful nights and the soul-sucking sleep deprivation.

My parenting discipline style toggles between good cop, bad cop, and unhinged. I work with my daughters on being kind. "If you see someone on the playground alone looking sad, go ask them to play," I tell them. I also sent them to Taekwondo to learn how to defend themselves against bullies, just in case. Even with the encouragement to be kind and the weekly physical training, they still spend an inordinate amount of time working on their insults, including, "You're not just a moron, you're a 'less-ron'" and "You look like a trashcan's grandmother." They cover all the bases, I suppose.

CHAPTER FORTY-THREE

REPUBLICANS OF GILEAD

When we bought our new house in Maplewood, construction took six months, so we all moved into Mom and John's town house at the Reston Town Center. Adeline was only six months old, and Audrey had just turned two. Dan and I slept in the basement with the cats. Three a.m. became the poop bewitching hour, when the smell of cat shit hit us like a ton of bricks, forcing us to get up, scoop poop, and walk it to the garbage can to deposit it outside. Despite the feline fecal factory, having Mom as a partner for meal planning and four adults in total to help clean up was pure heaven.

Audrey slept in her crib in Mom's sitting room, and Adeline slept in a crib in the guest room. John woke up at 4 a.m. each morning to catch the metro to work in DC, right around the time Adeline would wake up seeking comfort. Instead of rushing out the door and just letting me handle it, he'd pick her up and walk the hallway until she fell back asleep on his shoulder, forming the very special bond that makes Grandpa John her favorite. Being roommates, Mom and Audrey have a very special relationship too.

Mom and I constructed the most beautiful decorations for Adeline's first birthday party using a Pinterest board, which required more preparation and careful planning than my engagement party, shower, and wedding combined. We had the most fun together creating art as well as witnessing it, usually at concerts at Wolf Trap or the Reston Arts Festival or while traveling the world (pre-kids). Pinterest can be a very dangerous place.

The party went off without a hitch. I didn't do this for my oldest since her birthday is so close to Christmas, but she didn't seem to care; she's very low maintenance, whereas my youngest is obsessed with toys. We call her the "Inventory Queen," because she always knows where her belongings are at any given moment, and "Snoop," because she finds them before they're actually hers. I don't want to stifle the spirit of either one of my children. I want to keep the genetic fighter alive, which is very difficult to balance with the needs of everyone else. I just wish they had come with operating manuals.

Mom and John were a constant source of support and love for the girls. I don't know what I would have done without them. But after six months of village life, it was time for our fledgling family to move out. Moving day was on a day when, according to NASA, almost the entire earth, including the North Pole, was experiencing above-average temperatures, which made the separation a bittersweet and hot mess. Dan was hellbent on getting everything out of storage all by ourselves, so he refused to hire movers. We rented a giant U-Haul truck, which Dan and I loaded, along with my Jeep Cherokee and Mom's sixteen-year-old, black, stick shift Ford Ranger pickup truck (the smallest truck ever made). We all made about 14 trips to and from the storage facility and our new home in Maplewood.

While Mom was driving the pickup truck, she saw a shadow flying in the rearview mirror, but she assumed it was some kind of moving flag Dan had installed for her and the other vehicles. Two ladies in a blue sedan pulled up next to her and motioned for her to roll down the window on the passenger side. This was impossible to do without power windows, while she was in motion and as the only one in the vehicle, so the women made wide circular hand gestures. Mom could only make out, "EVERYWHERE! THEY'RE GOING EVERYWHERE!" which made her turn around to discover the white bureau in her truck bed had opened.

The thongs I had worn in my younger days were spilling out of the drawers like the flying monkeys in Elphaba's haunted forest castle. They were strewn and scattered all over both sides of route 50 near South Riding, and the item Mom had assumed to be a flag was actually one of my old wired, padded bras, size 34A, snagged by a floor lamp and fluttering in the wind, signaling the end of my thin, sexy days. Full-butt underwear was the only option from that moment on anyway, given the collateral damage of two pregnancies resulting in stitches where I tinkle, but the astral influence confirmed my granny-panty destiny. It is done. I will never be sexually attractive to a young person ever again.

———————

Growing up in Reston and living in Reston as an adult were two very different experiences. Overall, Northern Virginia is a rat race where industry put Reston on the map. Some say it's the real Silicon Valley; the largest suppliers of revenue are government, defense and aerospace, finance, science and health, and emerging technologies. There is always opportunity for work within a commutable distance. The traffic is horrible the closer you get to Washington, DC, and like most cities, the further away, the cheaper the cost of living. However, there are a plethora of wealthy neighborhoods in Northern Virginia.

I went for a visit to Maplewood based on a recommendation from a friend who worked as an executive for our builder. "Check out Maplewood," she said. "It's the best place in the area for you all to fit in." Much later (too late), I found out exactly what she meant. Maplewood was the epitome of "fancy meeting you here," lily-Mayflower-white. This was our first metaphorical red flag. The second was a literal red flag, erected by a neighbor who named his dog after a Nazi armored vehicle during the worst election year and outcome in US history, 2016.

My street in particular gave me the creeps. It was the perfect combination of the Republic of Gilead from *The Handmaid's Tale* and Stepford, Connecticut, from *The Stepford Wives,* as in the 1972 satirical "feminist horror" novel by Ira Levin, not the comedy movie remake starring Mathew Broderick and Nicole Kidman. I met most of my new neighbors at a Stella & Dot party across the street. The first one to approach me was a smug, poorly aging, brawny woman named Beatrice, who asked me right off the bat what I did for a living. When I answered, she asked, "Why work?" which I thought was super rude. She then guffawed and said, "That was my job back when I worked, a million years ago. So stressful!" I looked around the room for help and realized I was outnumbered. The only women with real careers on my street were the handful of absent liberals. I tried my best to keep my vitriol hermetically concealed for the remainder of the party.

Our neighborhood was still being built, and several unfinished lots had dumpsters stationed out front. So when I saw the Trump sign, I had to take a moment to recover from the dick-punch of realizing I now lived in the land of quackado. Then I posted a picture of it, linking it to a beautifully articulated speech by Michelle Obama damning Trump for bragging about sexual assault and mocking a reporter for having a physical disability. I also added my thoughts: "This sign belongs in the dumpster along with the person who put it up." A few hours later, I noticed a drop in my Maplewood Facebook friends, from 35 to 15. The ones who were left were there for the show and would post catty popcorn-eating memes and say shit like, "Let the racist people be racist in peace." All of this confirmed the sneaking suspicion that I'd inadvertently moved into a white supremacy ring.

The "flag war" had started before I moved in. It was between my Jewish and very vocal liberal friend, ironically named Karen, and the conservative majority of our streets. Instead of taking her to the mat with words in real life when she had questioned a neighbor for the reasoning behind his decision to pitch a Tea Party Gadsden flag on his front porch—a flag associated with a variety of conservative, pro-gun rights, and far-right political groups—the surrounding neighbors pitched four more alt-right flags.

In a podcast about a past boyfriend, Sarah Silverman (one of my favorite comedians) talks about how scary nationalism can be to Jews. She felt squeamish when he raised an American flag from his balcony. Flags are reminiscent of WWII in Nazi Germany, when all the swastikas started waving from porches and storefronts. Her podcast confirmed that I wasn't alone in feeling like the flags were more than just disturbing; they were a sinister reminder of the malicious nature of the far right.

The first neighbor to raise a flag was Liam Beagin, a mouthpiece for a notoriously incorrect radio show and the biggest conduit for misinformation and right-wing propaganda. When we first moved to the neighborhood, he seemed to be a reasonable guy. I had overheard conversations that made me question where he stood on many issues, but I was willing to have an open mind and be neighborly.

One night, while I was hanging out on Liam's deck, a Fleetwood Mac song came on the yacht rock station and I burst into song. Everyone was amazed, especially Julian, the only professional musician of the group, who asked me to be in his '90s cover band. I sent him a list of my favorites: 10,000 Maniacs and Natalie Merchant (since people think I sound just like her), Sarah McLaughlin, Sheryl Crow, The Cranberries, Sinéad O'Connor (a ton), Björk, Fiona Apple, Garbage, Jewel, Annie Lennox, Portishead, Mary J. Blige, Janet Jackson, Tori

Amos, Alanas Morrisette, and Suzanne Vega. He replied, "Jesus, this isn't the Lilith Fair!" Liam and John laughed. Apparently, Julian wanted me to only sing songs by The Cardigans. I shared my theory about the connection between child abuse and girls who speak or sing with high-pitched baby voices. He wasn't interested in continuing the debate or entertaining my theory, having two little girls himself and a hard-on for sweet sounding, mellifluous voices.

Over time, it became clear that Liam was just an unemployed pettifogger whose lavish lifestyle, subsidized by his trust fund, was tailor-made to appeal to Maplewood's receptive audience. His White fragility and subsequent fearmongering terrorized his neighbors, especially the ones who were just trying to make the world a better place for our children. His group of nuts sent mailers to everyone in the neighborhood with the message, "Your kids are being taught to hate you because you're White!" News trucks started coming around more frequently when Liam executed a strategy to remove liberal school board members, ban books, strip rights from the LGBTQ+ community and women, and ostracize all the reasonable members of the community, claiming Maplewood was a battle ground. Well, it is now.

In college, I discovered so many different people with contrasting views that I found a way to embrace differences and enjoy debates, knowing I was on the right side of history. To formulate a winning argument, I needed to learn more about religion. Politics were no different, and considering how close I lived to our government, I was ignorant. There is only so much you can learn from watching *Saturday Night Live*. Before 9/11 and T-dump, I assumed our country was in the hands of the experts and they could handle everything. Besides, I was just one voice, and I'd delayed registering to vote to circumvent jury duty, but then Al Gore chose Joe Lieberman, a Jewish man, for his running mate in 2004, and I started to pay attention.

It's a game changer when someone with your background becomes successful in the land of politics. Our rights as women have been dwindling every day since the inception of T-dump's political career and the GOP's Supreme Court takeover with dirty judges. Racist bigots and misogynistic pigs came out of the woodwork, materializing everywhere, emboldened by a tyrant and a right-leaning government. Maplewood seemed like an epicenter for all of this and reminded me of a direct quote from my beloved friend Bahija: "We've become a culture of disgusting people. We have a critical choice to make in order to satisfy the soul of America."

Knowing how much hard work needed to be done to hire and promote women and minorities into leadership and executive roles, I started to make changes of my own. I took on more projects to empower women at work, participated in the Women's March in DC, and canvased neighborhoods for the upcoming elections. It wasn't enough.

CHAPTER FORTY-FOUR

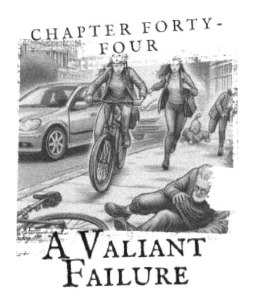

A VALIANT FAILURE

One afternoon, on my way to pick up the kids from daycare, I saw an older man, who had the same build and gray head of hair as my stepdad, lying on the side of the road between a parked car with a smashed taillight and a busted bicycle. I pulled over and ran up to him just as two other women did. The first was another good Samaritan named Jessica, who was already on the phone talking to an emergency dispatcher. The other was a nurse named Melissa, who I recognized because we had gone to South Lakes High School together. Nobody had seen the man fall, but his eyes were rolling to the back of his head and his face was turning blue. He was unconscious and sticking his tongue out, which, according to Melissa, was the body's response to running out of oxygen.

Jessica was receiving instructions through the dispatcher and calling them out to Melissa and me: "He needs fifteen pumps to the chest and two to the mouth!" The man wasn't breathing. He had a low pulse and was bleeding through the nose and mouth. I asked Melissa if she cleared the airway, remembering the CPR classes I took to become a certified Zumba instructor. "Yep," she said. "But I'm more worried his neck is broken." We all took turns trying to help but weren't sure we were doing it right. Each time I came in contact with his blood, I tried to spit it out. I didn't know until later about microshields, which are water-tight, tough plastic sheets with a built-in mouthpiece to act as a one-way valve or filter.

The EMTs showed up and took over. Melissa and I literally came up for air and could still taste his blood in our mouths. We decided to crack open a bottle of vanilla vodka that she had in her trunk, to gargle away the lingering unpleasant metallic flavor. Melissa followed the ambulance to the hospital since she still had time before she needed to pick up her son. We exchanged numbers so she could let me know how this would all play out. I was a half-hour late to pick up my kids.

During dinner, the captain of the county's fire and rescue department rang our doorbell to drop off some forms and let me know about the man's test results for HIV and hepatitis, which was common protocol. Thankfully, they were negative. Unfortunately, the man, who was named Edward Taylor, didn't make it to the hospital alive. Even though he perished, I'm grateful we were there to help. We were likely the three women responsible for his last breath on Earth. I take comfort in that. Even our futile attempts to keep him alive gave me a sense of how important it is, from one human to another, to connect and to do our best to take care of each other.

CHAPTER FORTY-FIVE

THE NOT-SO-PROGRESSIVE PARTY

Over the holidays, my friend Candy organized an ugly Christmas sweater progressive party, which was a four-course meal and accompanying drinks over six hours at four separate houses. Each host had two additional couples to help. The first house was for charcuterie and cocktails, the second was for apps and wine, the third was for the main course, and the last was for desserts, after-dinner drinks, and shots. I was thrilled to be selected for the last house, where we could break out our old DJ equipment and Jäger machine to make my favorite shots, Fuzzy Jäger Cranberries, more commonly known by a derogatory term aimed at females with red hair.

My friend Emily greeted each guest with a round of shots, and I played '90s hip-hop to get people dancing, which worked like a charm. I rapped "Gangsta's Paradise" on the microphone and crushed it. Everyone was laughing and having a great time, or so I thought. Upstairs, four of our male guests had found our life-size portrait of Barack Obama at the stair landing of our two-story living room. One of them was wearing a sweater with an upside-down snowman whose nose was a felt carrot protruding out of the face like an orange dick, which he lewdly stroked all evening. A liberal spy on one of the Maplewood conservative sites found a picture of him pretending to insert said carrot in Obama's mouth.

The week George Floyd was murdered, Emily organized a chalk-a-thon for the Black Lives Matter movement. Only six or seven homes displayed signs of love and peace on their driveways with chalk; the rest, in a coordinated effort through several exclusive social media channels, put up dozens of thin blue line flags along our street in a premeditated attack to outflank us. They went to events at wineries that displayed "Drunk Wives Matter" T-shirts on the wall, a stomach-churning play on words.

School shootings and sniper incidents, such as at the Jason Aldean concert in Vegas, were on the rise. My friend Robin and I organized a "Moms Demand Action" charity event at Café Montmartre in Reston. We were sick of just sitting around like ducks or fish in a barrel, doing nothing and getting more pissed off with every "thoughts and prayers" comment on social media.

After each mass shooting, Beatrice drove me bonkers by pitching a Second Amendment flag on her front porch. Sitting in my office, I could see it waving in my peripheral vision. While I was working so hard to advocate for women, she was taking us back in time. It was maddening. Her house was positioned directly in front of my office windows, so we purchased some flags of our own, including "Black Lives Matter," "We the People Means Everyone," "Science is Real," "Love is Love," and "Women Should Have Faculties Over Their Own Body." We also hung the Human Rights Campaign logo as well as an Irish flag, because both Dan and I are part Irish and we took a nice vacation there once to reunite with my old friend Caitriona!

We rotated the flags each month. Dan bought an anti-45 flag with a bright red diagonal slash going through the middle of the number 45, as in anti-45th President Donald Trump. It looked like a swastika from far away. I didn't put that one up, but I did unravel it one day in my front yard for Karen and asked, "What do you think?" She looked at it for a minute and said, "Well, it's spot-on."

Like a fishbowl, everyone could see into each other's glass houses, but I wanted to confirm my suspicion about how this particular flag might be offensive. Knowing we had one foot out the door since we'd already purchased our home in Fairfax County to be among more like-minded people and closer to my sister and mom, Karen said, "Isn't it liberating to be a woman with nothing to lose? Seems appropriate to me. You should put it up!" But that meant a ton of children would see something slightly resembling a swastika and, subsequently, parents would be forced to have conversations they might not be equipped or ready to have. I wasn't willing to do that to someone else. So I saved the flag for my departure and gifted it to the very same white supremacists who ruined Maplewood for me by erecting the Trump flag that made me feel so unsafe four tremendously long, grueling, and unhappy years earlier.

It was quite the paradox to live in such a beautiful community alongside a diagonalist, hateful milieu. I debated staying for the few liberal friends I had, like Emily and Karen, who I'd leave stranded to fight the good fight all on their own, but in the end, Maplewood took too much of an unhealthy toll on our family. Maplewood was supposed to be my Tanbark Drive, our forever home. We lived near the edge of a cul-de-sac, and prior to COVID-19 we were outside every day hanging with the neighbors, watching our kids play together. Then COVID happened and we stayed inside, while all these racist shitheads kept rearing their ugly, plain-featured, doughy-white faces.

When it was time to leave for good, I knew I'd be committing a crime (mail fraud) if I stuck the anti-Nazi flag in a Trumper's actual mailbox, so I put it underneath and drove through the community gates like I'd just escaped the force fields of a *Hunger Games* arena dome. But I left with a big smile on my face and without any need to look back.

A couple of days later, there was a post on the Maplewood community page: "The liberal left has gone nuts, and I will respond in kind with my 2nd Amendment right. Someone left me an anti-Nazi flag!" Some started to chime in: "Wait, isn't an anti-Nazi flag a good thing?" No response. Then the thin blue line ilk piled on, "What time did it happen? Who do you think did it?" They moved the conversation to a private page where they blamed Emily and ironically named Karen, but you guessed it, the flags are out of the bag now.

CHAPTER FORTY-SIX

SABBATICAL

I've spanned the gamut in the terrible bosses department. I had one manager who gave me spontaneous diarrhea every time we were scheduled to connect. I've had many managers who took my work and pawned it off as their own and those who motivated their teams with an unhealthy dose of fear and consequence. I've also had fantastic leaders who lifted me up and gave me a platform to lead myself and to make room for others to succeed.

In 2015, the small defense contracting company I worked for was bought by a bigger one, with duplicate overhead departments. My job would have been safe, but all my staff would have had to find new opportunities. I set out to find a new job by first reaching out to my network, and I landed an interview with Amazon Web Services (AWS) through a former coworker on the government side. During the interview, I informed my potential new boss that she must hire me since my oldest daughter's initials were also AWS and I needed the swag for her wardrobe. But in the end, I was selected for my experience and in-depth knowledge of security clearance screening practices.

I took on a demanding role that kept me on the phone all damn day! My time was spent prescreening and prepping potential candidates for interviews, and if they were successful, I negotiated salaries and closed the deal by offering them technical roles with the company. I loved walking through the halls the first day and seeing multiple private "mother rooms" on every floor, adorned with couches, a phone, and a place to work at a desk. Externally, my title was Sr. Client Lead, which was the highest level offered at the time, but internally we were called closers.

I caught myself delivering the identical spiel 8–12 times daily, like a robot, and opted to create a video of the repetitive information to save time for both myself and many others. The script went through two hundred iterations and took over two years to get approved through each department. Driving this process was a solo endeavor, and it made me realize that if I didn't do it, my vision of making the client lead role 30 percent more efficient would never come to fruition. I also worked with security to design a clearance status notification system. Once approved, the video was used to prepare over 33,000 candidates, and the system is still being used today. Then everyone started making their own videos, with a lot less red tape.

I wanted to step outside my comfort zone and stand behind others to drive change, so I volunteered for a board position at glamazon, an amalgamation of "Gay and Lesbian Amazon." I was the historian and archivist and helped organize events, took meeting minutes, and wrote newsletters. Today, AWS has over 136,000 employees. Each job has a corresponding document called Role Guidelines that determines each candidate's skill level at the interviewing and hiring stage and includes promotion criteria at the employee review stage.

There was no guideline available for closers and no path for advancement, so I wrote one myself. Getting it approved took a mountain of paperwork and required wading through another three years of bureaucracy, but in the end, a meeting with the most senior executives from all over the world was scheduled, and I was presenting. Despite my cross phobia, I made it another cross to bear, just like the video. At the end of the meeting, my boss asked, "So do we have your blessing?" The answer was yes, and I screamed, "Hallelujah!" I had finally created a path for myself and for others to move ahead. In general, these documents and exercises proved highly advantageous, empowering me to become a successful pioneer and instilling confidence in my ability to produce impactful written work.

Once my promotion to Principal Client Lead (the first of its kind) was complete, I listened to "Boss Bitch" by Doja Cat on repeat. I later moved into a recruiting strategist role. After seven long years of hard work and losing a significant amount of my sanity from stress, the threat of another recession loomed. Everyone at my level and below was offered a payout. I embarked on writing this book, labeling my time off as a "sabbatical" while retaining a good employment standing at work, with the fallback plan to return to Amazon should my aspirations of becoming an author fall through. Nevertheless, some friends and family members express worry that I may have divulged too much, potentially jeopardizing a return to prestigious corporate roles. We shall see.

CHAPTER FORTY-SEVEN

BURY ALL THE HATCHETS

Twelve years after I ghosted Sloane, while I was self-reflecting in order to start writing, the final season of *Ted Lasso* concluded. The message in the finale was about second chances, and it inspired a change of heart in me. I forced myself to relive our relationship and all the funny stories we shared. It made me remember how much we truly enjoyed each other. So, I wrote Sloane an email:

> "Hi Ronald,
>
> Hope you and your family are doing well. Not sure if you're a *Ted Lasso* fan. I certainly am. In the spirit of this meme below, I think 12 years is too long to harbor ill will. Please let me know your thoughts.
>
> —Carl"

The meme was a picture of Jason Sudeikis holding a tea cup and the words, "I hope that either all of us or none of us are judged by the actions of our weakest moments, but rather by the strength we show when and if we're ever given a second chance." I got a same-day response:

> "Helen!!! Carl:)
>
> Thank you for this. And of course I like *Ted Lasso*, and this meme is perfect. Twelve years *is* way too long. I'm so glad you wrote and hope your family is well too. Thank you for being the brave one and reaching out after all this time. I only have the best and funniest memories and have often regretted how our friendship stopped. I am sorry I wasn't there for you at your wedding and hope you can forgive me. Yes to second chances! I'm so happy to hear from you. Tell me things, you have girls like me! How's life stuff? What are you into these days?
>
> —Ronald"

Ronald and Carl, the names we had given each other all those years ago, had reconnected.

Then I found a naked picture of me, Jason, and Sloane in a shower, drunk and cleaning off debris from a food fight. I instantly ripped up the picture and threw it in the trash. When I told Dan about it, he said, "Well, why didn't you let me see it first?"

I applaud all the women in my story with the strength to be great mothers despite their lack of support from the adults or community surrounding them. It's a huge undertaking to break the cycle of abuse. I'm especially thankful for my mom and for Bahija, who both entrusted me with their deeply painful and heart-wrenching stories. After Mom's immediate family passed away, she found a way to establish new, healthy relationships with all my cousins, including Shannon and her three children. We all traveled across the state lines of Virginia, Pennsylvania, and New Jersey to meet up in Bethany

Beach, Delaware, for a reunion, proving it's never too late to mend fences.

Middle age has led to the emergence of a hairstyle reminiscent of a Fraggle: I have to draw eyebrows on my forehead daily and my neck hurts all the time . . . my neck and my back. I guess I'm already on the seventh stage of Erik Erikson's psychosocial stages of development: generativity versus stagnation. This is the part where I "make my mark" through creating something that will remain after I'm dead. Speaking of getting older, hot flashes started at around age 44, and are usually prefaced by a cold spell, like a warning. They last for a few minutes and make me feel like I'm being burned from the inside out; my skin turns bright red. The worst flare ups are always inconveniently triggered anytime I need to be on camera for work. During COVID, this was also accompanied by my daughter's refusal to be on camera for "synchronous learning", and when the teachers asked her a question, she'd say, "Can't you just ask someone else?" and go back to drawing on the floor.

Unfortunately, hot flashes aren't a problem I can just scratch off, like a plantar wart. Ask any gynecologist or obstetrician why they have only a four-hour optional workshop offered in medical school to learn about menopause even though women spend at least one-third of their lives in menopause. Seriously, I'd like to know the answer.

Growing up, I felt personally responsible for my sister's survival. I wanted to toughen her up, to prepare her for the ugliness of the world, and was sometimes a little too harsh. I felt like the best person for the job since she was Holly High School and I was a juvenile delinquent destined for prison. Coincidentally, she's the one who forced me out of my maternity pants well after I gave birth. Without her, I'd probably still be wearing jeans with an elastic top. What goes around, comes around. I'm still 20 pounds overweight, and all jeans give me an unsightly muffin top, while she's in the prime of her life.

Though Julie is my younger sister, people often mistake our birth order because she's three inches taller than me, acts more mature, is more diplomatic, and is always three steps ahead in life's game of chess. I can't count how many times she's helped me resolve professional and personal conflicts with her exceptional mediator skills. I'm a good negotiator and problem solver, but she's the CEO of our family and I'm the second-in-command, just like Audrina was all those years ago. Unless Mom's around. Then I'm the lowest on the totem pole; basically dog food.

I might have been a hell raiser, but I always wanted a normal life. Despite my lack of blind faith in a higher power, the concept of angels watching over us all is very appealing. I could have easily ended up just like Aunt Caroline on the fateful Halloween night of my car crash over 30 years ago. Perhaps it was she who shifted me into the passenger seat of the car hurtling along at 40 miles per hour.

I'm still fighting for my version of the nuclear family I lost in my childhood and craved for the remainder of my development into adulthood. I created my own family, just like the one I longed to be part of, except I'm the captain now. I just wanted to slip that in while also conveying that I'm the one making the decisions. I'm now able to frame my past experiences as what happened *for* me instead of what happened *to* me, which has shaped me into the person I am today.

I've also cultivated a top-tier friend network, my fr-amily. Several are first- or second-generation Americans, a conscious choice of mine to avoid ethnocentrism—you know, just in case it's possible to single-handedly thwart the next Holocaust. I've specifically sought out friends who live outside America for a chance to go visit people in other countries. Friends have come to see me here in Fairfax County, and I've introduced them to my world. In reciprocation, they have been able to introduce me to the people and places that are important to them. It's almost like an adult version of playing "You show me yours; I'll show you mine."

Comparable to my efforts to include non-Jews in our Passover tradition, to make a good impression on the world outside of my bubble, I also want to decimate the spread of white supremacy, like the kudzu unfurling all over I-80 like a contagion. I'll have you know, reader, that you've been spared six chapters on "How to Catch a Nazi" by one of my editors. Summarizing here, I want to be proud to live in this country again because we course-corrected, we chose correctly, and we moved forward instead of backward. And I hope that this year (2024), the good guys win the battle for the soul of America.

I'd love to become a centenarian, just like Reston's founder Bob Simon. At the very least, I want to be able to look back on this book and be proud of how much I've grown since writing it. I want to pay it forward and protect the underdog, continuing to be a voice for those who don't have one, aren't comfortable being loud, or lack the courage to be angry. I've been described as a highly dependable friend whom others can rely on, and I seek friends who are equally steadfast and reliable in return. The more I can safeguard people around me against injustices, the more justified I become.

My insecurities as a child at my cousins' bat and bar mitzvahs made me feel all alone; Julie and I were the only ones without our parents. We didn't have our family unit anymore. Yet even in those moments, I'd always find a way to enjoy myself, to make sure Julie was having fun too, and then things didn't always seem so bad. That ability to be the life of the party—even if that means on my own—is a gift, and I would never have developed that skill if I hadn't experienced and come to understand that vulnerability.

In college I learned about the latest version of the *Diagnostic and Statistical Manual of Mental Illnesses*, which serves as an essential reference for psychologists, equivalent to a bible for a preacher. The publication is also used by professors, researchers, psychiatrists, drug regulation agencies, health insurance and pharmaceutical companies, the legal system, and policy makers. While writing this book, I wondered what my particular diagnosis was all those years ago when I was a patient of Dr. Farber. I looked him up (or "searched him up," as my kids say) and found him at the Reston Psychological Center as a partner and clinical psychologist. I sent an email to the office with a picture of myself around the age I'd undergone treatment:

Subject: Inquiry

Hello. I'm a former patient, from 40 years ago, of Dr. Edward Farber. I would love to set up an appointment to ask him some questions. Could you please ask him if he remembers me? If so, I'm happy to pay for an official appointment.

Thanks, Ellen

I kid you not, Dr. Farber remembered me! During our virtual appointment, I shared my gratitude. Doctors aren't required to keep records for more than seven years. He must have been a teenager when he treated me. I summarized my trauma to help jog his memory: "My parents divorced, and I acted out by getting violent with my sister, Julie." I told him his treatment inspired both Audrina and me to major in psychology. He wrote this down. Perhaps for his next book?

Before I became his patient, Dr. Farber cared mostly for victims of child abuse. When he noticed similar symptoms of trauma from kids going through a separation or divorce, it surprised him. For my diagnosis, he chose the most innocuous code because he worried about all the kids who'd eventually go on to work for three letter agencies in the area; he used a Z code, which represented "product of family tension." Basically, my parents' divorce was the primary issue, and I acted out as a result. I was seen once a week for a year but then sporadically after that.

I was really closed-up and spent an inordinate amount of time covering up my real feelings of anger by pretending to be happy, stoic, or emotionless. I asked him how he got me to open up, and his answer was completely logical, but for some reason it made me burst into tears. He said, "After providing gradual support without judgment, I gave you the tools to show your frustration, like drawing or toys. In the beginning, I'd make interpretive statements like, 'Wow, it must be awfully hard to go from one house to the other all the time.' You would notice how I put words into how you were feeling, which helped you to tell me what was really bothering you." I felt my throat tighten and started crying like I was nine years old again. It was terribly embarrassing.

What he remembered most was my anger. "Today, there are 10-year-olds refusing to participate in split custody; they'll just refuse to go," he said. "That could have easily been you." I thought about how much I absolutely cherish my mother now. We always have fun together. There is nothing better than craft days with my mom ("Grammy" to the kids). I can't even function when we argue. This made me realize how far we had come and how incredibly lucky I am to have her in my life, and so close.

Helping my children navigate relationships can be really tricky. The difficulty is deciding when to step in and when to let them stand up for themselves. I aggressively encourage my girls to take care of each other and foster their bond as sisters. I'm relentless because when I'm dead and gone, they'll only have each other. I leverage my relationship with Julie as a good example of an end goal. I need them to be there for each other in those moments of vulnerability—to grow together, like Julie and I have, instead of apart.

We chose to come back to Fairfax County to be close to family and a lifetime's worth of building a network of friends here. When my brother comes down from Pennsylvania for a visit, we bond over our similar tastes in music and comedy, such as Jeff Buckley and Fern Brady. Brandon is a fantastic singer as well.

My sister ended up picking out our new neighborhood for us by buying and designing her own custom home in a neighborhood where the model home was still on the market. "It's got all the bells and whistles," she said. "Each bathroom is blinged out, all the light fixtures, appliances, and flooring are top of the line, and everything is upgraded. You should check it out!"

"Are you sure you want us that close? The girls are going to want to walk over and spend lots of time with you," I said.

"That's exactly what we want!" she replied cheerfully.

I didn't even need to see it—I was sold. Our dreams of hosting family reunions and grand Passovers together were finally coming true.

At the walk-through, I remembered my 300-square-foot, fifth-floor walk-up in NYC and how ecstatic I was to purchase the 1,200-square-foot, two-bedroom condo when I moved back home to Reston, which felt like a palace in comparison. Deep down, all I ever wanted was just a little place to rest my head, one that I could call home and where I could make *my* peanut butter and jelly sandwiches, like Wendy Beamish in *St. Elmo's Fire*.

Julie always wanted kids but focused on her career until she found her magical prince, which took longer than expected. Being close to her nieces was her way of adapting to life's unfair circumstances. She would have been a wonderful mother, better than me for sure. Moving across the street was the best end of the deal for everyone.

I stood in the backyard, looking up at the new builder's model, soon to be my home, on the .89-acre lot surrounded on two sides by tall trees from the seventy-year-old park behind us. I never thought I'd have a fancy new house so close to nature. Tears welled in my eyes. I thought, *Could this slice of heaven really be mine someday?* I cashed out enough of my stocks for a down payment and put the plans in motion. We were finally becoming a part of the upper middle class, a moment I'd coveted since third grade.

"And now?" you ask? My slice of heaven is covered in garbage. My children behave like wild animals, dropping shit wherever they go. Sometimes literal shit. They blame the dogs or an imaginary culprit they aptly named "the dirt rat."

I want to end this book with love. In the end, or the middle since I'm hoping to live to be one hundred, I've enjoyed the roller-coaster ride as much as arriving at the destination. I'm still learning. I'm still struggling to exit the merry-go-round of negativity. All of us, from cradle to grave, are a work in progress. When we bought this house, Dan and I had high-paying jobs. Now that I'm unemployed and the payout has run dry, I'm starting to question whether we made the right decision. I miss my house cleaners, who quit because of the dirt rat.

Dan is the engineer I've always wanted, my magical prince who embodies all the fantastic traits of my beloved Pop Pop. I trust him completely, mostly because he's an introvert who never wants to leave the house or do anything without me. However, Dan doesn't like parties or socializing in groups larger than four, and I absolutely adore parties; hell, I'm the life of the party! I'm a night owl and he's an early bird. But because I had a high-powered career and the kids are doing better with a routine, I have acclimated to his senior citizen sleep schedule and banished my club-promoter-from-the-'80s mentality. Marriage is very hard, but wading in the unfairness of it does me no good. Being grateful is so much easier.

Audrina will always be my closest friend, and technically my relationship with her is the longest one I'll ever have other than with my family. We still talk on the phone for hours, even after months or sometimes whole seasons have passed by, but never years. We've always had a milestone of some kind to share at least once a year; sometimes wonderful, sometimes terribly heartbreaking. She makes me see things more clearly. More importantly, she makes me feel like myself again when I've strayed too far. It's like taking a dose of psychedelics every time I talk to her. I'm centered back to my authentic self.

The struggle to keep everyone I love close is a battle I'll fight for the rest of my life. Dad and LeeAnn live a couple of hours away, but we don't see each other nearly as much as I'd like, and I suffer from chronic disappointment as a result. Julie has become a master at lowering and managing her expectations. "You can't change people, Ellen. Just take what you can get and try to enjoy it," she says with the self-preservation of a tardigrade, the most resilient animal in the universe.

My mom lives close by and helps out immensely with the kids, as does Julie. We go on vacations and celebrate every holiday together, and we host epic Passovers. Mom is friends with our friends, comes to our happy hours, and is the first person I selfishly hugged two months into COVID, because I couldn't bear to be stuck in a bubble without her. We still bicker and have our moments of strife. Writing this book and balancing everyone's feelings and specific recollections of the past has been very challenging. I don't shy away from confrontation, but I still have feelings that are easily hurt, even though I'm an adult. Arguing with each other dampens our spirits, leaving us joyless until we reconcile. I don't have everything figured out, but I know I will keep fighting for my family. I won't give up.

My kids are my second chance for new adventures. And some say true adventure is making yourself so miserable that the experience is worth sharing with others. I want to guide my kids toward being the wonderful people they have all the potential to be and to learn from them how to be the best mother I can be. I'm excited to watch my children learn about the world and make me take another look, to see it anew through their eyes and impart to them the wisdom I've obtained from the people, places, and experiences of my half-century of living.

Like my underwear, my life has evolved in ways I never imagined. Who would have thought that the little girl parading around the neighborhood in her Wonder Woman undies would eventually be the same woman who spits in the face of injustice in her granny panties! The sexy thongs may be a thing of the past, but the rebel lives on.

We each have a fighter within us. Mine showed up very early in life and not in the most refined fashion. But every fight I was in as a teenager shaped me into the outspoken, candid, and compassionate grown-up I am today. I hope all the troublemakers reading this feel less alone in the world and are inspired to persevere and keep fighting the good fight.

Again, like wearing underwear, the choice is up to you.

ACKNOWLEDGMENTS

The year 2024 happens to be the 60th anniversary of Reston and the 230th anniversary of the founding of the University of Tennessee. As someone raised in Reston, I always recognized the town's uniqueness, yet it wasn't until I ventured elsewhere that I truly appreciated its value. I am profoundly thankful to the University of Tennessee and New York City for aiding me in discovering my aspirations. It took residing far from home and exploring diverse locations to affirm my beliefs, solidify my identity, and realize my preference for the convenience of a car and the short trips to local stores. I am immensely thankful for the opportunity I have been given to explore and define my identity and purpose. These environments were instrumental in shaping my path of self-discovery. I am proud to declare myself a suburban individual, and Reston stands out as a remarkable suburb.

Throughout the various stages of my socioeconomic journey, I experienced both setbacks and growth while residing in Reston. In hindsight, the most pivotal moment of my personal development emerged from what initially seemed to be the worst phase of my life. The necessity of moving out of my sizable family home during the equal custody arrangement following my parents' divorce ultimately led me to meet Bahija, who became not only my neighbor but also my friend, mentor, and guardian, ultimately becoming a transformative and essential figure in my life. Bahija, your silent endurance of unimaginable trauma, merely doors away from my home, has impacted me in ways that transcend words. Your courage and strength are a testament to the indomitable human spirit in the face of adversity. Our connection, nurtured through art, love, and a shared longing for belonging, has been a wellspring of inspiration for me, shaping the person I have become. I eagerly anticipate reading your upcoming memoir, *Black Girl Tragic*, and pledge to cheer you on as your most ardent supporter.

To all my friends at the Reston Community Center, thank you for welcoming me into your community with such warmth and openness. I don't know what I would have done without my happy place. Your support has been my rock this past year, as have been all the connections I've formed, including with my wonderful editor Malka Wickramatilake, my typesetting guru, Risa Ryan and my fabulous headshot photographer Rachel Walisko. Special thanks to the very first friends I met, Laura, Kate, Scarlett and Kathleen, for all our joint projects and to my teachers Shruti, Trish, Kate and Tena who were so phenomenally patient with me. And to Jim, thanks for the new magazine and quote about adventures.

Malka, you are exceptionally lovely. Thank you for reading my original 175,000-word journal about everything that has ever happened to me in my entire life and for having the patience and expertise to pull out the diamonds from the rough. I know there were a lot more rabbit holes and turds than gems. I am incredibly grateful for your steadfast support and the multifaceted roles you have assumed in this journey. To me, you have been a savior, friend, therapist, cheerleader, and even a telepathic editor. Our meeting feels fated, as if our connection transcends this lifetime. Your knack for enhancing my words has not only made me sound more intelligent but also uplifted me in ways beyond measure. Thank you for being such a significant presence in my life.

To my former defense contracting and Amazon work Amazon friends, I'm so happy for the friendships and long-lasting lessons from our journey together.

To my exceptionally talented graphic designer, Keegan Eichelman, I want to express my heartfelt appreciation for your patience, dedication, and for consistently delivering outstanding work. Your ability to handle all the revisions and feedback with grace and creativity is truly commendable. Thank you for your hard work and for always providing the most exceptional product.

To Margie Bernknopf and Sue Caley, thank you for being such wonderful friends to my mom and for always supporting me as well.

To Angie Dickinson, thank you for taking me under your wing all those years ago and for being such a constant source of support. Also, thank you for scoring the boat ride with Bob Simon for Mom, Jules and me!

To my forever best friend Adrienne Bernknopf Group, thank you for encouraging me to forgo the kids' book to write this one instead. I adore your sensitive heart and your clever wit, and you will forever be the angel on my shoulder, guiding me and supporting me through it all.

I extend a heartfelt appreciation to Erica Cohen Eden for her generosity and exceptional design prowess. The captivating cover of this book is entirely attributed to your creative talent!

A special thank you to Melinda Arons and Robert Goudie, who possess the most intriguing careers. Your support means the world to me, and I am grateful to have you both in my corner.

Thanks to Leigh Snitiker for being my first set of eyes. I hope I "killed all my darlings" from the original manuscript, based on your valuable feedback.

To Cynthia Shang and Shantha Ramachandran, thank you for diligently rectifying the many grammatical and chronological errors and enhancing the overall coherence of the text. Your attention to detail and editorial finesse are truly commendable—I could easily envision you excelling as professional editors.

To Mina Song Palkindo, thank you for encouraging me to make every word count and ensuring there was a payout in the end.

To Caitriona McCarthy, Andrea Büring, and Sonja Hoffman, thank you for letting me use your real names and for being the coolest international friends a girl can have.

To my dear old neighbors Emily Morford and Karen Jimmerson, I deeply apologize for leaving you on the battlefields alone. Your resilience and dedication to the cause inspire me. Please know that my support and solidarity are unwavering. Keep fighting the good fight, and remember, I stand by your side every step of the way.

To the esteemed authors who generously gave me their time to walk me through their process, including Kristina Alcorn, who wrote the beautiful book about Bob Simon called *In His Words,* and Watt Hamlett, who wrote the kids' book I wanted to write first, *Reston A-Z.* Also to Chuck Cassio and Danny Olmes, your guidance has been invaluable as I navigated the realms of storytelling.

I would like to express my gratitude to all individuals who participated in interviews and provided valuable perspectives and enriching content. I extend a heartfelt thank you to my cousins Shannon Carlino, Nick Curl, and Tommy Curl, as well as to Heather and Mike Blum, Sharon and Mickey Safra, Michelle Rosenberg, Mike Waetzman, Ted Lichtenfeld, Susan Raucher, and my sister-in-law Robbe Bressot and brother-in-law Larry Price. Additionally, my thanks go out to my friends Sommer Seneca, the O'Connors (also known as the good Pats), Lyn Corrado Pugh, Amanda Brent, Holly Harris, Caitriona McCarthy, Dave Jannerone, Wild Bill (who requested anonymity), Joey Archer, Gail Toth, Katie Deninger Vandervalk, Mary Sherrill, Kelly Ladd, Kim Eisler, Emily Matson, Nathalie Lupien, Jason Marshall, Joy Lee Higdon Spencer, Sharon Shumaker, Kate Teachout Richardson, Gwen Alexander, Monica Miller, Dr. Edward Farber, Larry Carnahan, Bahija (Franqi French), Bobby Graham, Ashish Dhir, Lalitha Ganesan, Brad Strader, Peter Nester, Justin Niessner, and Molly Marshall Curry.

To the Issa family, the move across the street brought with it the joy of meeting my lifelong friends, the Bernknopf's (Bernadotte's in the book). Misook, your physical prowess is truly inspiring to me. I deeply appreciate your efforts in helping me stay fit during the challenging times of COVID-19. My affection extends to your entire family. John, I am grateful for your unwavering friendship with Dan. Logan and Lincoln, your positive influence on the girls as role models doesn't go unnoticed. I hold each of you dear to my heart. Much love to you all!

Special thanks are also extended to my aunts Lorrie and Joanne. In particular, I want to acknowledge my uncle Kurt, whose poignant account of escaping the Holocaust with his mother has significantly impacted my worldview. His story has left an indelible mark on my perspective and serves as a powerful reminder of resilience and courage in the face of unimaginable adversity.

I hold a deep love and appreciation for my brother Brandon, and my quasi stepbrothers, Johnny & Simon. The opportunity to expand my family and share profound connections with you fills my heart with joy and gratitude.

I'm sorry, Kendal Kain, Ronnie Beets, Steve Georgopolis, Kenny, Marshall, Tony, Laith, Uncle Ed, Aunt Pat, Uncle Tommy, and Aunt Caroline, for missing your funerals. Though I was unable to pay my final respects in person, you hold a special place in my heart that will endure forever.

To my current friends/influencers, Misook & John Issa, Josh Katz & Jenny Shtipelman, Bethy Gallagher, Laura Ebert Harman, Amy Rohrbaugh, Alexis Norton, Joanna Harris, Sara Bell & Nick Pasquini, Dawn & Kristen Cunningham, Monisha & Kevin Lucier, Bridget & Gresan Kraja, Robin Griffin & Casey Grubs, and Liz, thank you for the endless inspiration, meaningful conversations, and unforgettable moments we have shared over the past few years.

To Shanon-Rose Griffith, I extend my heartfelt gratitude for consistently motivating me three times a week, reminding me of who I am and encouraging me to put one foot in front of the other. Your guidance instills in me a sense of strength and competence with each session. I appreciate how you skillfully divert me from my troubles with engaging trivia and amusing tales about your wonderfully hilarious family.

To my esteemed publisher and friend, Jenn T. Grace, I express my heartfelt gratitude for your unwavering belief in me and your invaluable knowledge throughout this remarkable journey. Your exceptional intellect and unwavering support have been instrumental in my success. I am profoundly grateful to have crossed paths with you, thanks to Malka and your book, Publish Your Purpose. I am grateful to Mike Zall for addressing all my legal inquiries with both altruism and expert acumen. To my project manager Chris Agnos, thank you for your steadfast assistance with everything, therapy sessions, and first-class guidance. Mostly, thanks for keeping me on track!

I am grateful for the unwavering support extended by Alex Campbell of the Reston Museum. Your assistance during numerous unexpected visits and calls has been truly invaluable, and your consistent helpfulness is deeply appreciated!

To my dear cousin Shannon, I am immensely thankful for your patience and willingness to candidly address all my personal queries. Reconnecting with you and bringing our families together brings me immense joy. Your presence in my life is a true privilege.

To my husband Dan, thank you for your patience with my flair for the dramatic. Life is truly enriched with you by my side. Your thrifty habits in saving the money I might have otherwise spent on clothes are greatly appreciated. Never stop making up ridiculous lyrics to popular songs. I know your love language is to grab my boobs. It's about time someone noticed I have them. You are still my magical prince, and you will always be Handsome Dan. I am immensely grateful to my husband and children for their steadfast support throughout the past year and a half. Their patient ears and understanding hearts as I shared daily updates about the book and expressed the challenges of the revision process mean more to me than words can convey.

To my cousins in the Heit family, Brad, Scott, and Mark, thank you for marrying me . . . I mean, er, thank you for the role you played in orchestrating my marriage. I love you, your spouses, and your children very much.

To my stepparents, John and LeeAnn, your enduring love for both my parents and me has truly been the cornerstone of our family's stability. John, special thanks for doing my taxes and picking up the dead bird on the stairs so I could enter my condo in Reston.

To Jeff & Melinda, thank you for being such wonderful parents to Dan, and the only parents willing to drop off groceries when Dan, Audrey and I all had a stomach flu, and I was pregnant with Adeline. You all are the best in-laws on the planet.

To my first nuclear family, my sister Julie, my mother, and my father, thank you for standing witness to my journey through the trials and tribulations of coming of age, and thank you for taking my daily phone calls or answering my random texts about what year I played soccer, in which year was I diagnosed with a learning disability, and so on. Your willingness to share our collective stories and maintain hope in my growth means everything to me. I love you all immensely, and your spouses too!

To anyone inadvertently omitted from my acknowledgments, please know that it was unintentional. Your presence and impact are valued, and I extend my gratitude to all who have touched my life in meaningful ways.

BIBLIOGRAPHY

B., Ruth. "Lost Boy." Self-produced and first performed on Vine. Recorded 2015. Track 6 on Safe Haven. Columbia and Sony, EP.

Bel Canto. "Shimmering Warm and Bright." CD. Oslo: Crammed Discs, 1992.

Belle, Blu Lu, Hawkins, James, and Johnson, Barbara Anne. "Iko Iko." The "Iko Iko" Story (American Folk) featuring Belle, Blu Lu, Hawkins, James and Johnson, Barbara Anne, ACE, 1953.

Blige, Mary J. "Real Love." What's the 411?, Uptown, 1992.

Camp Sunshine. (1984). Retrieved from https://www.campsunshine.org/

Cool featuring L.V. "Gangsta's Paradise." *Gangsta's Paradise*, Tommy Boy Records, 1995.

DiFranco, Ani. In Living Clip. Righteous Babe Records, 1997. Audio CD.

Doja Cat. "Boss Bitch." *Birds of Prey: The Album*, Atlantic Records, 2020.

Edie Brickell & New Bohemians. "Circle." Produced by Pat Moran. Recorded 1988. Track 6 on Shooting Rubber Bands at the Stars. Geffen Records, vinyl.

Eiffel 65. "Blue (Da Ba Dee)." Europop, Bliss Corporation, 1999.

El Paso." Gunfighter Ballads and Trail Songs, Columbia Records, 1959

Ella Fitzgerald. "Ella Fitzgerald Sings the Harold Arlen Songbook." "Paper Moon" 1961, Verve Records.

Fleetwood Mac. *Greatest Hits*. Warner Bros. Records, 1988. Audio CD.

Fleetwood Mac. Rumours. Warner Bros., 1977

Fried, Joseph P. "Club Owner Charged with Arranging Drug Parties." New York Times. March 21, 1997. https://www.nytimes.com/1997/03/21/nyregion/club-owner-charged-with-arranging-drug-parties.html.

Friedkin, William, dir. The Exorcist. 1973; Burbank, CA: Warner Bros., 1998. DVD.

Hickox, Anthony, dir. Hellraiser III: Hell on Earth. 1992; Los Angeles, CA: Miramax, 1992. VHS.

Joel, Billy. "The Longest Time." An Innocent Man, Columbia, 1983.

Joplin, J. (1971). Me and Bobby McGee [Recorded by Janis Joplin]. On Pearl [Album]. Columbia Records. (1971).

Led Zeppelin. "Ramble On." Produced by Jimmy Page. Recorded June 1–2, 1969. Track 7 on Led Zeppelin II. Atlantic Records, LP.

Kerman, Joseph. *Listen*. 9th ed. New York: Bedford/St. Martin's, 2014.

Madonna. "La Isla Bonita." True, Sire Records, 1986.

Metallica. "Wherever I May Roam." On Metallica. CD. Elektra Records, 1991.

Mozart, Wolfgang Amadeus. Rondo Alla Turca, K. 331.

Newton, Juice. "Queen of Hearts." Juice, Capitol Records, 1981.

Nugent, Ted. "Stranglehold." Produced by Tom Werman and Lew Futterman. Recorded 1975. Track 1 on Ted Nugent. Epic Records, LP.

Raitt, Bonnie. (1972). Love Me Like a Man [Recorded by Bonnie Raitt]. On Give It Up [Album]. Warner Bros. Records. (1972).

Raitt, Bonnie. "Love Me Like a Man." Give It Up, Warner Bros. Records, 1972.

RUN DMC. *Raising Hell*. Profile Records, 1986.

Sandler, Adam. "The Hanukkah Song." What the Hell Happened to Me?, Warner Bros. Records, 1996.

Sheb Wooley. "One Eyed, One Horned, Flying Purple People Eater." The Purple People Eater, MGM, 1958.

Stravinsky, Igor. "The Rite of Spring." Composed in 1913.

The Beatles. "Hey Jude." On The Beatles 1967-1970. CD. Apple Records, 1973

The Story. "Angel in the House." On The Story. CD. Elektra, 1993

Withers, Bill. "Lean on Me." Still Bill, Sussex Records, 1972.

Webber, Andrew Lloyd. *Evita: The Complete Motion Picture Music Soundtrack*. MCA Records, 1996. Audio CD.

Wonder, Stevie. "I Wish." Songs in the Key of Life, Tamla, 1976.

Yazoo. "Situation." Upstairs at Eric's, Mute Records, 1982.

Zelda by Yellow #5, 1998

ADDITIONAL RESOURCES

Articles

- Ebola Reston Outbreaks: https://virus.stanford.edu/ filo/ebor.html Kudzu: The Invasive Vine That Ate the South": https://www.nature.org/en-us/about-us/ where-we-work/united-states/indiana/stories-in-indiana/ kudzu-invasive-species/

- https://www.theguardian.com/film/2010/sep/20/ Robin-williams-worlds-greatest-dad-alcohol-drugs

- "Parallel Owner Responds to Criticism over 'Drunk Wives Matter' T-shirt": https://www.loudountimes. com/news/parallel-owner-responds-to-criticism-ove r-drunk-wives-matter-t-shirt/ article_f71be28e-af30-11ea-982c-67dbf325d1ec.html

- "The Shifting Symbolism of the Gadsden Flag" by Rob Walker: https://www.newyorker.com/news/news-desk/ the-shifting-symbolism-of-the-gadsden-flag

- "The Day Ebola Was Almost Released on U.S. Soil": https://www.dailymail.co.uk/news/article-272115 7/25-years-ago-different-Ebola-outbreak-Va.html.

- "25 Years Ago in Virginia, a Very Different Ebola Outbreak: https://www.cbsnews.com /new s/25-years-ago-in-virginia-a-v ery-different-ebola-outbreak/ The Truth About Your Horoscope, https://jokedroll. tripod.com/Jokes/Your_Horoscope.htm

- Stravinsky's Riotous 'Rite of Spring': https://www.npr. org/2008/03/21/88490677/stravinskys-riotous-rite-of-spring#:~:text=Stravinsky's%20music%20is%20 famous%20for,of%20the%20dancers%20on%20stage.

Books

American Psychiatric Association. *Diagnostic and Statistical Manual of Mental Disorders, Fifth Edition.* Washington, D.C.: American Psychiatric Association, 2013.

Atwood, Margaret. *The Handmaid's Tale*. Boston: Houghton Mifflin Company, 1985.

Behrendt, Greg, and Liz Tuccillo. *He's Just Not That Into You*. New York: Simon & Schuster, 2004.

Haley, Alex. *Roots: The Saga of an American Family*. New York: Doubleday, 1976.

Hayes, Isaac. *Cooking with Heart and Soul*. New York: Atria Books, 2000.

Klien, Jesse. *I'll Show Myself Out*. Publisher: Harper Audio, 2022

Levin, Ira. *The Stepford Wives*. New York: Random House, 1972

O'Connor, Sinéad. *Rememberings*. New York: Houghton Mifflin Harcourt, 2021.

Patterson, James. *Cat and Mouse*. New York: Little, Brown and Company, 1997.

Rememberings: Scenes from My Complicated Life by Sinead O'Connor

Thomas, Marlo, and Friends. *Free to Be...You and Me*. New York: McGraw-Hill, 1974.

Movies and Television Shows

Anchorman: The Legend of Ron Burgundy." Directed by Adam McKay, performances by Will Ferrell, Christina Applegate, Steve

Carell, and Paul Rudd, DreamWorks Pictures, 2004. Boiler Room, directed by Ben Younger Dexter, created by James Manos Jr. Duffer Brothers. "Stranger Things." 2016–. Netflix.

"Have It All." *30 Rock*, season 1, episode 16, NBC, March 8, 2007.

Parenthood. Directed by Ron Howard, performances by Steve Martin, Mary Steenburgen, Dianne Wiest, and Keanu Reeves, Universal Pictures, 1989. Film.

Reservoir Dogs, directed by Quentin Tarantino

Roots, produced by David L. Wolper

Ross, Gary, director. *The Hunger Games.* Performances by Jennifer Lawrence, Josh Hutcherson, and Liam Hemsworth. Lionsgate Films, 2012.

"Scrooged." Directed by Richard Donner, 1988. Paramount Pictures.

Sudeikis Jason, creator. *Ted Lasso.* Performances by Jason Sudeikis, Hannah Waddingham, Juno Temple, and others. Apple TV+, 2020-present.

Seinfeld: The Nap." Seinfeld, created by Larry David and Jerry Seinfeld, directed by Andy Ackerman, season 8, episode 18, Castle Rock Entertainment, 1997.

Sex and the City." Created by Darren Star, HBO, 1998-2004.

South Park, created by Trey Parker and Matt Stone

St. Elmo's Fire. Directed by Joel Schumacher performances by Emilio Estevez, Rob Lowe, Andrew McCarthy, Demi Moore, Judd Nelson, Ally Sheedy, and Mare Winningham, Columbia Pictures, 1985. Film.

Splash, directed by Ron Howard

"Something in the Air." 90210, directed by Stuart Gillard, written by Scott Weinger, aired October 1, 2008, The CW.

The Boss Baby 2: Family Business*. Directed by Tom McGrath, DreamWorks Animation, 2021. Film.

The Exorcist: Directed by William Friedkin, performances by Ellen Burstyn, Max von Sydow, Linda Blair, Warner Bros., 1973.

The Heartland Series, produced by WBIR-TV in Knoxville, Tennessee.

"The Leftovers." Created by Damon Lindelof and Tom Perrotta, HBO, 2014-2017.

"Where Everybody Knows Your Name." Cheers, performed by Gary Portnoy, written by Gary Portnoy and Judy Hart Angelo.

"Yellowjackets." Created by Ashley Lyle and Bart Nickerson, performances by Melanie Lynskey, Juliette Lewis, Christina Ricci, Showtime, 2021.

Videos

Christina Pazsitzky, TikTok post, 5/23/2024, https://www.tiktok.com/@christinap/video/7236864689018342699?lang=en, "aw I want to be an 80's mom".

"My Neck . . . My Back . . . My Neck and My Back!" 2021 TikTok post by be.safe.tho: https://www.tiktok.com/@be.safe.tho/video/6989266809996266757

Petty, Tom. "Don't Come Around Here No More." Directed by Jeff Stein, MCA Records, 1985.

Sarah Silverman 'Felt Very Weird,' 'Scared,' 'Shaken' By Seeing American Flag Flown in Yard https://www.newsbusters.org/blogs/culture/lindsay-kornick/2017/12/07/sarah-silverman-felt-very-weird-scared-shaken -seeing

Sexual Harassment and You, SNL, https://www.youtube.com/watch?v=PxuUkYiaUc8

"The Reston Story," a YouTube video by the Reston Museum: https://www.youtube.com/watch?v=Qn5eHyn51nY

Saturday Night Live, "Delta Delta Delta: Finals Week": https://www.youtube.com/watch?v=VZi_fkdfXm0

ABOUT THE AUTHOR

Ellen holds a bachelor's degree in psychology and music from the University of Tennessee. With professional experience spanning 36 years, she entered the workforce at a young age, overcoming legal barriers. Her career path led her through industries rife with the prevalent misogyny of the era, a challenging narrative vividly captured in her compelling story.

At Amazon, Ellen's proactive initiatives led to groundbreaking promotions amid the challenges of the COVID-19 pandemic. Her dedication to fostering diversity and innovation, showcased through her work, embodies a leadership style aimed at positive change. Ellen is a highly sought-after strategist, speaker, coach, and trainer. She also specializes in guiding individuals on nurturing troublemakers and the ability to define constructive rebellion.

Ellen's memoir resonates with readers by infusing humor and introspection, encouraging them to confront life's uncertainties with laughter and many adaptive course corrections. Ellen spends her free time with her husband and two daughters; her very demanding Coton de Tulears, Niles and Frasier; her sister Julie and brother-in-law Larry, who live across the street; and her mother and stepfather, who still reside in Reston, Virginia, less than a half-hour away.

Connect with Ellen:

Website: Ellenrbsmith.com
Email: ellen@ellenrbsmith.com
Instagram: https://www.instagram.com/suburbantroublemaker/
YouTube: https://www.youtube.com/@suburbantroublemaker
Facebook: https://www.facebook.com/SuburbanTroublemaker/

Podcasts: TBD

THE B CORP MOVEMENT

Dear Reader,

Thank you for reading this book and joining the Publish Your Purpose community! You are joining a special group of people who aim to make the world a better place.

What's Publish Your Purpose About?

Our mission is to elevate the voices often excluded from traditional publishing. We intentionally seek out authors and storytellers with diverse backgrounds, life experiences, and unique perspectives to publish books that will make an impact in the world. Beyond our books, we are focused on tangible, action-based change. As a woman- and LGBTQ+-owned company, we are committed to reducing inequality, lowering levels of poverty, creating a healthier environment, building stronger communities, and creating high-quality jobs with dignity and purpose.

As a Certified B Corporation, we use business as a force for good. We join a community of mission-driven companies building a more equitable, inclusive, and sustainable global economy. B Corporations must meet high standards of transparency, social and environmental performance, and accountability as determined by the nonprofit B Lab. The certification process is rigorous and ongoing (with a recertification requirement every three years).

How Do We Do This?

We intentionally partner with socially and economically disadvantaged businesses that meet our sustainability goals. We embrace and encourage our authors' and employees' differences in race, age, color, disability, ethnicity, family or marital status, gender identity or expression, language, national origin, physical and mental ability, political affiliation, religion, sexual orientation, socioeconomic status, veteran status, and other characteristics that make them unique.

Community is at the heart of everything we do—from our writing and publishing programs to contributing to social enterprise nonprofits like reSET (www.resetco.org) and our work in founding B Local Connecticut.

We are endlessly grateful to our authors, readers, and local community for being the driving force behind the equitable and sustainable world we are building together. To connect with us online or publish with us, visit us at www.publishyourpurpose.com.

Elevating Your Voice,

Jenn T Grace

Jenn T. Grace
Founder, Publish Your Purpose